COOK
FIGHT

ALSO BY KIM SEVERSON

Spoonfed:
How Eight Cooks Saved My Life

The Trans Fat Solution

The New Alaska Cookbook

ALSO BY JULIA MOSKIN
AS COAUTHOR

American Brasserie

Butter Sugar Flour Eggs

Gale Gand's Short and Sweet

Gale Gand's Just a Bite

The Campagna Table

Patricia Yeo: Cooking from A to Z

Bistro Latino

Boy Gets Grill

Bobby Flay Cooks American

COOK FIGHT

2 COOKS, 12 CHALLENGES, 125 RECIPES

AN EPIC BATTLE FOR KITCHEN DOMINANCE

JULIA MOSKIN & KIM SEVERSON

with a foreword by FRANK BRUNI

photographs by EVAN SUNG

ecco

An Imprint of HarperCollinsPublishers

All photographs by Evan Sung except for the following:

pages 3, 4, 7, and 11 by Rebecca McAlpine

HarperCollins books may be purchased for educational, business, or sales
promotional use. For information please write: Special Markets Department,
HarperCollins Publishers, 10 East 53rd Street, New York, NY 10022.

FIRST EDITION

Designed by Suet Yee Chong

Library of Congress Cataloging-in-Publication Data has been applied for.

ISBN 978-0-06-198838-7

12   13   14   15   16   IND/RRD   10   9   8   7   6   5   4   3   2   1

We dedicate this book to all the strong-willed cooks who have come before us, fighting to their last breath over whether there should be pork in the meatballs or raisins in the stuffed cabbage

CONTENTS

FOREWORD

by **FRANK BRUNI**

Y ou show me a cookbook worth relishing, and I'll show you one that's about a lot more than food.

Sometimes the larger theme—the *über*overlay—is only flickering in the margins, dancing in the background of all those enticing ingredients, all those mouthwatering pictures. It sneaks up on you, whispering rather than shouting its presence.

And sometimes, as with *CookFight*, it's loud and proud and front and center. This is a book about friendship, in all its salty, sweet, and sour glory. The jousting herein, the part that provides the second syllable of the title, isn't solely or even mainly between recipes, though there are recipes galore, and they are fine, accessible ones that you'd be foolish not to try and wasteful not to put into heavy rotation. It's between personalities, sensibilities. It's the clang and clash of two people enjoying and lamenting and working through their different approaches to, and perspectives about, both cooking and life.

In the pages that follow, the two of them do their own terrific job of introducing themselves. So let me talk here about my own experience of them. A culinary metaphor is probably in order, given that what you hold in your hands belongs—if I may be briefly highfalutin—to the genre of culinary arts, and given that the three of us met and got to know one another in the Dining section of the *New York Times.*

Julia and Kim were my ciabatta, and I was their prosciutto. That is to say, they sandwiched me. Julia sat in the cubicle to one side of mine, Kim in the cubicle to the other. I was in the middle.

And I was in the middle too—stuck there, *caught* there—at the beginning of *CookFight.*

As Americans adjusted to a long, grinding economic downturn, those of us in the Dining section frequently discussed how the *Times*'s food coverage could best reflect and respond to it. The idea to have Julia and Kim each do a small, multi-course dinner party on a tight, unyielding budget came up.

As we refined the idea, we decided that the exercise should be a contest of sorts, to make the doing of it and thus the reading of it livelier. And there should be a judge. And the next thing I knew, my role as the newspaper's restaurant critic had landed me in that hot seat.

I had to pick a winner, and thus a loser.

Giving one half of the ciabatta a crown, and the other half the back of my hand.

Suffice it to say that these were the first two dinners that ever gave me indigestion before, not after, the actual eating.

Off to Kim's I went. She was then living in the Park Slope section of Brooklyn, on the ground floor of a lovely townhouse, and we moved from the living room to the dining room as she staged a Mexican fiesta of sorts, replete with canapés and assemble-your-own tacos. She was clever, that Kim. She camouflaged her tight budget with extra work and a bounty of flourishes and fillips: chile-spiced peanuts, pickled onions, two kinds of homemade salsa, homemade slaw. That's Kim. Ever spirited. Ever inventive. Ever fun.

I gorged on everything she made, with a song in my stomach—but also a knot. There was no way Julia would outdo this. And she was going to hate me something lethal when I gave Kim the nod.

Off to Julia's I went. She had just moved into a new apartment on Manhattan's Upper West Side, and I was getting my first glimpse of it. Two stories, river views: lovely place.

And lovely meal. Oh, what a lovely meal. If Kim's had a special kind of gusto, Julia's had a particular kind of grace.

She presented homemade gougères. She served a velvety soup—more of a bisque, really—with tomato and cumin in it. A perfect salad was followed by a perfect pasta dish. The courses had a very proper rhythm, until dessert, when she punctuated the end of the meal with the epicurean equivalent of a childish giggle, combining tangerine and vanilla into what was essentially a Creamsicle float. That's Julia. Very much the lady, but with a mischievous streak just under the skin.

So what did I do?

You saw this one coming: I declared a tie.

I suspect some of you would have favored Kim's feast; others, Julia's. And that may be your experience of the book they've produced, organized around a series of cook-offs, a sequence of good-natured battles. Who can do the better comfort food? The better children's meal?

One obvious payoff of this approach is that you get two storehouses of recipes in one, doubling your counsel and pleasure. But the less obvious payoff—and for me the bigger one—is that you get a dialectic. A dialogue. A conversation whose participants are as resourceful and engaging as any you'll find. You can trust me, because that prosciutto-dom of mine? It lasted more than three years, all of them extraordinarily happy ones.

CookFight celebrates Caesar salad and onion dip and black beans and smoked salmon and pots de crème and all the rest of it, rummaging exuberantly through a diverse larder and nudging you—no, *tugging* you—toward the stove. And it also celebrates the way two very different people can forge one very special bond. It's delicious.

ACKNOWLEDGMENTS

The authors are grateful to the *New York Times* and its remarkable staff, especially Jill Abramson, Rick Berke, Trish Hall, and our dining section family. Legendary food writers Marian Burros and Florence Fabricant taught us so much: How to stare down editors and publicists alike, and how to survive the annual Thanksgiving issue. Special props to Sam Sifton, who hired both of us; Pete Wells, who edited the first *CookFight* stories; and Frank Bruni, whose idea it was. And a from-the-foxhole kiss to Vivian Toy and Eric Asimov, who watched our relationship unfold from neighboring cubicles.

Being acquired and edited by publisher Daniel Halpern at Ecco is a writer's dream. Thanks also to editor Libby Edelson, interior designer Suet Chong, art director Allison Saltzman, designer Steve Attardo, and managing editor Joyce Wong. We appreciate and adore our photographer Evan Sung: his gentle patience, his sensitive images, and his tips for making our hands look good in photos.

Additionally, from Kim: This book rests on the generosity of all the people who took the time to teach me to cook and to write. Very big thanks and praise to my delicious daughter, Samantha, and my family in all its forms.

You have been generous with your love, even when I had to stay at the keyboard too long or asked you to try dishes that still needed work. A special thank you to Leslie. And, especially, thanks to Julia Moskin, without whose friendship I would not have survived my early days in New York. She is the model work wife and always, always has my back.

Additionally, from Julia: There would be no words on the page if not for my dear husband, Darren, who took the kids away for the weekend when I had to write, made gallons of salad dressing and poached dozens of eggs, and kept me well supplied with paper towels and love. Billy and Kate are, as always, the lights of my life—especially while they were eating artichokes. My parents were good-humored about the multiple home invasions this book required of them. Elizabeth Marshall has gracefully picked up the slack for me on more occasions than I can count. Kim Severson, my work wife, has showed me what it is to be a food journalist, a newsroom shark, and a true friend.

INTRODUCTION

We'll never forget our first fight. It wasn't over food, although by then we had already argued plenty about mayonnaise, Mexican food, and the impact of industrial agriculture.

The fight was born of the kind of tense situation that comes up when reporters collaborate on a story. Kim was in the weeds on a deadline and Julia offered help, then bailed at the last minute without apology. There was slamming of phones, searing silences, maybe some crying in the bathroom. It wasn't about the work. It was about loyalty.

That's because we were always more than coworkers. We were work wives.

Everyone needs a work wife—that one person at the office who always has your back. Your work wife is who you really spend your days with, who listens to you when you're on the phone with your mother, who knows that you like your coffee just barely sweet, who orders your lunch when you are cranking out a page-one story on your birthday. When you're away on vacation or a business trip, your work wife makes sure you don't miss important news and gossip from the workplace (especially when it's about you).

The office can be a cold and lonely place, but a work wife makes it manageable.

We got hitched in 2004, when we were both newcomers at the *New York Times*

Dining section. Julia was largely clueless as a journalist and had spent more weeks in France than in all the flyover states put together. But she knew restaurants and New York City, her hometown, where she had the dirt on every chef, bagel, and ball of falafel. Kim was an experienced food reporter with a Pulitzer nomination under her belt. She had lived all over the country, including a long stint in Alaska. She had serious news chops and talked big, but she was secretly intimidated by the city and the notorious politics of the *Times* newsroom.

And there was more. Kim is gregarious, athletic, and ambitious; Julia, a hater of exercise, meetings, and competition. Julia was raised Jewish, Kim, Catholic (both with reservations). Julia is straight; Kim is gay. Julia loves her martinis and manhattans; Kim doesn't drink.

It took only a few weeks before we realized that our opposite backgrounds were going to result in an intense friendship. And a few years after that, that friendship produced the articles that were the seeds of this book.

Throughout our long stint in a shared foxhole at the *Times,* we helped each other eat better and pushed each other to improve. "What am I going to do with that pork shoulder I took out of the freezer this morning?" one of us might ask during a moment of work avoidance. Or, "I think this needs lime zest or something, don't you?" the other would say, offering a forkful of a dish she'd brought for lunch that day.

But these were not always pleasant conversations.

We soon realized that we almost never cook the same thing in any given situation. It often turned out, for example, that what Julia considered a great party dish for kids, Kim found incredibly boring. Or that what Kim thought was a deeply felt homage to her grandparents struck Julia as unnecessarily complicated, and greasy besides. Julia mocked Kim's love of turkey. Kim scoffed at Julia's angst over a pending dinner party for ten.

Basically, we argued about what to eat all the time, and we got paid to do it. But that fighting also reminded us of how to have fun in the kitchen, even on the hardest days. And of how much we loved having someone else who understood exactly why good food matters and how hard it often is to find. We were both working mothers with spouses and deadlines and doctor's appointments and parents to worry about. We shared a love for eating and a lack of time for cooking. This book tells the story of those years.

THE BUDGET CHALLENGE

JANUARY

THE BUDGET CHALLENGE

---

by KIM SEVERSON

Our first challenge found us creating a dinner party for six for $50. There were only a few rules in our culinary Thunderdome. Pantry basics like spices, butter, and olive oil didn't count toward the total price. And guests would bring the wine or liquor.

Oh, and there was one more thing. Frank Bruni, the restaurant critic of the *New York Times*, would come to both dinners and write a critique of each one. The day you get handed an assignment like that is the day you wish you had called in sick. But, as the kids say, game on.

Bring it, Moskin!

I started thinking about pork shoulder, a versatile cut that can be braised into all sorts of main attractions. But I didn't want to create the kind of Ital-Cal meal that is my default style. Besides, Frank has spent a lot of time in Italy. He is Italian-American, for heaven's sake. Anything less than a stellar pasta would mean certain defeat. And if I knew Julia, she was going French. Well, here in Brooklyn, baby, we were heading south. I figured if I looked toward Mexico, I could make clever use of inexpensive ingredients like jicama, beans, and peppers. If I combined them with big flavors and artisan techniques, I could easily come in under the $50 mark. Julia would fold like a cheap tent.

The heart and soul of my strategy would be a big pot of carnitas perfumed with oregano, orange zest, and the delicate Mexican cinnamon called canela. As a bonus, the carnitas came with a built-in coach. The recipe belongs to Tara Duggan, who writes a column called "The Working Cook" for the *San Francisco Chronicle* and has a cookbook out with the same name.

I knew, though, that I had to elevate the carnitas from a pot of long-simmered pork into something special enough for a dinner party. "I'm going to make my own tortillas and serve them hot off the griddle," I told Tara.

She gasped. Brilliant! OK, she didn't actually gasp. But she did remind me that trying out an untested dish on guests is never a good idea. So I spent the entire weekend before my party rolling out practice tortillas. I was not going down over a tortilla. And I was certainly not going to fail in front of Julia Moskin. This was war, and sacrifices had to be made.

The meat for the carnitas posed a challenge. I buy pork at my food co-op or at a farmers' market. Because of the way these pigs are raised, it's very expensive.

Unless I split a chop six ways, that kind of pork was not going to fit into my budget. So I headed to the local Pathmark, where the picnic roast—the lower part of the shoulder—cost $1.49 a pound. Even better, the four-pound one I bought was covered in skin. This led to my next genius move.

I had already planned to set out a series of Mexican bar snacks for appetizers. I figured variety would make up for the lack of luxury ingredients. I had stumbled across a recipe for spicy candied peanuts in a new book called *Simply Mexican* by Lourdes Castro. I added lime juice, zest, and chili powder to jicama, and set out the pepitas I bought already roasted. And for the centerpiece of my little snack tray? Homemade chicharrones from the skin of that grocery-store pork. (Cut the skin into inch-wide strips. Season, set in a roasting pan, and cover with an inch of water. Bake at 400 degrees until the fat is rendered and the water has evaporated. Stir now and then.)

My tray of Mexican snacks cost less than $5, which left a little money for a second appetizer. I cut some store-bought tortillas into wedges and fried them up. (Take that, $4 bag of tortilla chips!) Then I searched for the cheapest, sturdiest, freshest fish I could find to make ceviche. Atlantic tilefish was only $7.99 a pound.

For a little extra flourish, I threw thin slices of red onions into white vinegar spiked with Mexican oregano and refrigerated them overnight. The pickled onions and my two inexpensive blender salsas would be perfect with the carnitas.

But tacos alone would not be enough. My original plan had been to stew some dollar-a-pound pinto beans cowboy-style, with canned tomatoes, onions, peppers, and chorizo. But I realized I could afford $4 for a pound of big, gorgeous Rancho Gordo Christmas lima beans.

For something refreshing, I turned to that budget star, cabbage. I dressed up two different kinds with a confetti of watermelon radishes and raw poblano peppers, then tossed the slaw with Coach Duggan's cilantro-lime vinaigrette.

By this point, I had abundance on my side. But I needed to stick the landing if I was going to beat Moskin. After toying with a cake that called for a cup of expensive pecans, I hit on it: a dark, spicy gingerbread with soft whipped cream and dulce de leche.

The only thing I needed to buy for the cake was molasses and eggs. For the dulce de leche, I used an old trick: I submerged an unopened can of sweetened condensed milk in water and simmered it for 2½ hours. I let it cool, opened the can, and boom, dulce de leche for $3.

(You don't literally want it to go boom, so make sure you keep the can completely covered with water while it cooks.)

The night of the party, I was flinging masa like a tortilla machine and freaking out when Coach Duggan called.

"Don't forget to relax and let the food take you where it wants to go," she said. "This is about enjoying the process and the food and your guests."

Note to self: never pick a coach from California again.

But she was right. The tortillas were hot and delicious, and her carnitas didn't let me down. I had come in $2.45 under my $50 budget, and everyone seemed to be having a great time. Especially Frank, who was spooning up the dulce de leche like a schoolboy with a bowl of pudding.

I was sure victory was mine.

Then I heard that Julia was planning a move so brilliant and confident that it immediately knocked me off my game. She was going to serve pasta at her party.

CHILE-SPICED PEANUTS

This snack delivers a lot for a little effort. The only trick is the timing when you toast the peanuts.

1 cup unsalted roasted peanuts

3 tablespoons sugar

1 teaspoon cayenne pepper

1 teaspoon kosher salt

6 lime wedges

To toast the peanuts: Heat a nonstick skillet over high heat. Add the peanuts and shake the pan often so that the nuts toast slightly but do not burn. After about 2 minutes, you should begin to smell the aroma of toasted nuts. Remove the nuts from the pan and set aside.

To make the spice mixture: Set the pan over medium heat. Sprinkle in the sugar, cayenne, and salt (be careful, because the heated cayenne can cause some coughing). Allow the sugar to melt slowly, stirring lightly and frequently with a heatproof spatula. As soon as all the sugar has melted, return the peanuts to the pan and stir to coat well with the sugar mixture. The peanuts may clump a bit, but that is OK.

Turn the spiced nuts out onto a sheet of parchment paper. Allow the nuts to cool and the sugar to set.

Serve with wedges of lime for guests to squeeze over the nuts as they eat them.

Makes 1 cup

TACOS DE CARNITAS

The fresh tortillas made this meal particularly amazing. There are simple recipes using store-bought masa. Or seek fresh ones at a market with Mexican ingredients. If you use store-bought corn tortillas, warm them briefly in a hot dry pan and wrap in slightly damp, warm tea towels to serve.

3 pounds pork shoulder
  (butt or picnic)
5 cups water
7 strips orange zest
1 large onion, chopped
5 garlic cloves, chopped
1 cinnamon stick, preferably
  Mexican canela

2 bay leaves
1½ teaspoons crushed dried
  oregano, preferably Mexican
1½ teaspoons kosher salt, plus
  more to taste
1¼ teaspoons red pepper flakes
¼ teaspoon ground cloves

FOR SERVING
24 small corn tortillas, warmed
Chopped fresh cilantro
Finely chopped onion
Fresh Tomatillo Salsa (recipe
  follows)

Roasted Tomato Salsa (recipe
  follows)

Trim any thick fat from the outside of the pork. Cut the meat into 1-inch cubes; discard any cubes that are pure fat.

Put the pork in a large pot. Add the water, orange zest, onion, garlic, cinnamon, bay leaves, oregano, salt, red pepper flakes, and cloves. Bring to a boil, then reduce to a simmer. Skim off any scum that has formed on the surface. Simmer for 1½ hours, or until the pork is very tender, adding more water if necessary to keep it submerged, and skimming off the foam.

Season the pork with salt. Bring to a gentle boil and cook until the water has evaporated, about 30 minutes.

Cook the pork a little longer to fry the meat slightly, or cook it longer if you prefer crisper meat. Stir often and add a bit of water if the meat sticks or seems about to burn. Remove the bay leaves and cinnamon stick.

Fold a few tablespoons of carnitas inside each tortilla and top with cilantro and onion. Serve the salsas on the side.

Makes 6 to 8 servings

Fresh Tomatillo Salsa

I thought making fresh salsas was some kind of secret, magic skill I would never possess. This and the following recipe, adapted from *Simply Mexican* by Lourdes Castro, proved me wrong.

1 pound tomatillos (about 9), husks removed, rinsed, and quartered

2 jalapeños, stemmed and halved lengthwise

1 cup lightly packed fresh cilantro leaves and tender stems

1 garlic clove

½ onion, chopped

½ teaspoon kosher salt

2 tablespoons water

Combine all the ingredients in a blender and pulse a few times, then blend into a puree.

The salsa can be stored in an airtight container in the refrigerator for up to 2 weeks.

Makes about 1½ cups

Roasted Tomato Salsa

2 heaping cups cherry tomatoes, halved

2 jalapeños, stemmed and halved lengthwise

1 small onion, quartered

2 garlic cloves, not peeled

2 tablespoons olive oil

Salt and freshly ground black pepper

¼ cup red wine vinegar

⅓ cup water

Preheat the oven to 400 degrees. Line a rimmed baking sheet with parchment paper or aluminum foil.

Place the vegetables cut side up on the baking sheet. Drizzle with the oil and season generously with salt and pepper.

Roast for 30 to 40 minutes, or until the tomatoes have shriveled and developed deep brown spots of color; do not allow the vegetables to char.

Remove garlic skins, transfer the vegetables to a blender, add the vinegar and water, and puree until smooth. Taste the salsa and adjust the seasoning if necessary.

The salsa can be stored in a tightly covered container in the refrigerator for up to a week.

Makes about 1½ cups

POBLANO-CABBAGE SLAW

This slaw can take a lot of different forms. The cabbages can change—napa or red or green—as can the radishes. I like big red ones, or those colorful watermelon radishes that are red and pink to their heart. The key is to shred the cabbage uniformly and to give the dressing more than a moment to meld into the vegetables.

FOR THE SLAW

½ small head green cabbage
½ small head savoy cabbage
1 medium watermelon radish or
    1 bunch red radishes

2 poblano chiles
1 green apple, such as Granny
    Smith

FOR THE VINAIGRETTE

3 tablespoons fresh lime juice, or
    more to taste
½ cup minced fresh cilantro
¼ teaspoon kosher salt, or more
    to taste

Freshly ground black pepper to
    taste
Pinch of cayenne pepper
¼ teaspoon sugar
3½ tablespoons vegetable oil

To make the slaw: Remove the tough outer cabbage leaves and core the cabbage. Using a food processor, a mandoline, or a knife, shred the cabbage as fine as possible.

Peel the watermelon radish, if using, and cut into matchsticks, then cut the matchsticks in half. Alternatively, trim the red radishes and roughly chop. Stem and seed the chiles, then chop into pieces smaller than a dime. Core the apple and cut into the thinnest matchsticks you can.

Mix all the ingredients together in a large bowl. Set aside.

To make the vinaigrette: Whisk together all the ingredients except the oil in a small bowl. Let the cilantro steep in the mixture for a few minutes, then whisk in the oil in a steady stream to emulsify.

Taste and add more lime juice, salt, and/or pepper if needed.

Pour the vinaigrette over the slaw and toss well.

It's best if it sits for a ½ hour or so. Serve.

Makes 6 to 8 servings

DARK MOLASSES GINGERBREAD

This recipe, adapted from *The Gift of Southern Cooking* by Edna Lewis and Scott Peacock, is really about the best cake I know. It always works, people love it, and it just gets better with age. All the flavors of the spices meld and the texture gets more like a steamed pudding. Serve it with freshly whipped cream.

A simple, albeit risky, way to make dulce de leche begins with a can of sweetened condensed milk. Remove the label, place it in a saucepan, and cover with water. Bring it to a boil and simmer for 2½ hours. Be very careful to keep adding water. If the water evaporates completely, the can might explode. If you have a slow cooker, pour the milk into half-pint canning jars, cover, place them in a slow cooker and cover with water. Cook for about nine hours.

2 cups all-purpose flour
2 teaspoons baking powder
¼ teaspoon baking soda
1 teaspoon ground cinnamon
½ teaspoon ground ginger
½ teaspoon salt
8 tablespoons (1 stick) unsalted
  butter, cut into pieces
1 cup boiling water
2 large eggs, lightly beaten
1½ cups dark molasses

Preheat the oven to 350 degrees. Place oven rack in center of oven. Butter and flour an 8-by-8-by-2-inch baking pan.

Sift the flour, baking powder, and soda into a large bowl. Blend in the spices and salt with a whisk.

Melt the butter in the boiling water and whisk into the flour mixture.

Add the eggs to the mixture, along with the molasses. Whisk until well blended and pour into the preared pan.

Bake for 35 to 45 minutes, or until a skewer plunged in the center comes out with no trace of raw batter.

Makes one 8-inch square cake, about 8 servings

THE BUDGET CHALLENGE

by JULIA MOSKIN

Her fifth appetizer was like a knife in my heart. When Severson and I were set the challenge of making dueling dinners for six for $50—about the least one can spend on dinner for two in a Manhattan restaurant—I was, frankly, not concerned. As many readers know, a decent cook with a deep bench of pantry ingredients can easily make a great meal with $50, or even $5, if necessary.

Then I sat down at her table, and the icy reality of competition sank in. She was playing to win: her meal was big, delicious, and interesting. By the time she'd served a ceviche of tilefish, marinated in lime juice and triumph and spooned onto a homemade tortilla chip, I knew I would have to sweat as never before.

And, by then I was also mad. Severson accused me of lacking the fighting spirit. She comes from a family of hardworking dairy farmers and Olympic skiers. In mine, a game of Scrabble and an errand is considered a full day, and I have shunned competition since going down in the first round of the 1977 New York City spelling bee. Cooking skills would not determine the victor. We are both enthusiastic home cooks, not trained chefs. My only chance lay in rock-solid menu planning.

This called for a revisit to the Museum of Bad Ideas: mistakes in recipe choices or

execution that I hope never to make again. A dessert recipe from Jean-Georges Vongerichten that called for thirteen Granny Smith apples, peeled and thinly sliced. (I still have hand cramps.) Steak au poivre for eight in a freshly painted white kitchen. (I still have smoke stains.) Embracing simplicity by serving a platter of naked steamed vegetables and a bowl of mayonnaise for dinner. (We had to order Chinese food afterward.) I spent a couple of hours surrounded by grease-stained cookbooks and clippings, recalling the peak of my lentil soup years, the best lamb stews of the 1990s, the finest lemon cake in living memory.

But would lentil soup impress? Could it win?

"What's the one best thing I have ever made?" I demanded of friends and family, soliciting only flattering details of my past.

The answers proved my suspicion that French or Italian classics, combined with some twists on American tradition, would be popular. (It works for Thomas Keller.) That approach would also enable me to buy some key ingredients at Costco, where basic luxuries like nuts, cheese, and dried fruit are good and cheap.

I paired the flavors of tomato soup and grilled cheese sandwiches: a cold soup made with canned tomatoes and a huge hit of cilantro, that suggests but beats out gazpacho, and gougères, buttery egg-cheese puffs that make the house smell great. As a fan of cheddar, especially in melted form, I was happy to inject it into a French recipe for gougères that I've made many times with expensive Gruyère, Roquefort, and Parmigiano-Reggiano; it performed admirably.

Now the menu needed something crisp and refreshing after the salty, cheesy pleasures of the appetizers. I was committed to using supermarket produce, but a trial run of celery salad did not go well. ("Not everyone," said my husband, choosing his words carefully, "likes celery as much as you do.") Tender, pale, ever-so-slightly-bitter hearts of escarole were perfect with a basic puree of anchovies, garlic, lemon, and olive oil.

Roast chicken is widely beloved, but it has been played to death (it's the Adele of entrées). I knew it could not win on its own. Then I remembered a curiously satisfying experience I'd had with a recipe from Claudia Roden. I'd enjoyed ripping up a roast chicken with my bare hands—carving is so finicky and leaves so much behind—and mixing it with pasta, pine nuts, currants, and rosemary.

As someone who can eat an entire bread basket or many gougères during the ravenous stage before dinner arrives, I am not usually hungry by the time dessert rolls around. But in a cookbook by the Los Angeles chef Suzanne Goin, I found a speck of a recipe that sounded like a very upscale Creamsicle float (fresh tangerine juice, homemade vanilla bean ice cream). I bought a bag of not-pretty but in-season tangerines for $3. Knowing I couldn't afford a vanilla bean, I found an ice cream recipe that called for vanilla extract, and I bought extra-delicious, all-natural heavy cream to compensate. (As it turned out, a pint of this grass-fed elixir costs more than Häagen-Dazs in the market where I shop.) Served with a straw and a spoon, topped off with a cap of seltzer bubbles, the dessert was a smashing, dirt-cheap success.

COLD TOMATO CILANTRO SOUP

This Moroccan soup, adapted from Mediterranean food goddess Martha Rose Shulman, is a clever twist on gazpacho, with unexpected flavors.

1 large or 2 small bunches fresh
  cilantro
3 tablespoons olive oil
1 large onion, chopped
2 large or 3 small garlic cloves,
  chopped
¼ cup tomato paste
1½ teaspoons ground cumin

1 teaspoon paprika
Pinch of cayenne pepper
One 28-ounce can tomatoes,
  whole or diced, with their liquid
4 cups water
Salt and freshly ground black
  pepper
1 lime, halved

Pull off a small handful of cilantro leaves to use for garnish and set aside. Tie the remaining cilantro into a bundle with kitchen twine.

Heat the oil in a medium deep heavy pot over medium-high heat. Add the onion and cook, stirring, until softened and golden, about 8 minutes; reduce the heat as needed to prevent browning. Add the garlic and cook, stirring, for 1 minute. Add the tomato paste, cumin, paprika, and cayenne and cook until the tomato paste begins to darken, about 2 minutes.

Add the tomatoes with their liquid, the water, salt and pepper, and the cilantro bundle and bring to a boil. Lower the heat, cover, and simmer for 30 minutes. Remove from the heat and let stand until cool enough to blend.

Remove the cilantro bundle. Using a regular or handheld blender, blend the soup until smooth. Refrigerate until very cold, at least 4 hours, or overnight.

Just before serving, squeeze in the juice of half the lime and add salt and pepper to taste. If desired, squeeze in more lime juice. Serve in small bowls or cups, garnished with the reserved cilantro leaves.

Makes 6 to 8 servings

1. Cooking the dough; it will be lumpy when the flour is added.

2. When it clumps and pulls away from the sides, the dough is cooked.

3. Add the eggs one at a time.

4. Beat hard until the dough is soft and oozy.

5. Use a pastry bag or a thick plastic bag with a corner snipped off for piping. Grasp the bag above the dough, hand over hand like a baseball bat.

6. A little browned peak on the top of each puff is very appealing.

CHEDDAR GOUGÈRES

French gougères are usually made with Gruyère cheese, but these soft puffs are just as good made with American cheddar. In fact, they can be made with any hard cheese lingering in the refrigerator, or a combination of cheeses. There is simply nothing better with a glass of wine—sparkling, white, or red.

1 cup water	4 large eggs, at room temperature
8 tablespoons (1 stick) unsalted butter, cut into pieces	1½ teaspoons dry mustard
½ teaspoon salt	¼ teaspoon cayenne pepper
1 cup all-purpose flour	1½ cups shredded sharp cheddar cheese (about 6 ounces)

Preheat the oven to 375 degrees. Line two baking sheets with parchment paper or nonstick baking mats.

Combine the water, butter, and salt in a medium heavy saucepan and bring to a boil. Turn off the heat, add the flour, and mix with a wooden spoon until the dough starts to pull away from the sides of the pan and come together. Set aside, without stirring, for 5 minutes.

Add the eggs one at a time, mixing well after each addition. With each addition, the dough will look glossy and slick at first; let it come together before adding the next egg. Mix in the mustard, cayenne, and cheese. The dough will be quite loose and sticky.

Scoop up a heaping teaspoon of dough and use another spoon to scrape it onto one of the lined pans; it should form a mound about an inch in diameter. (Alternatively, use a pastry bag or heavy plastic bag with one corner cut off to pipe small mounds onto the pan.) Repeat with the remaining dough, leaving ½ inch between the puffs.

Bake for about 25 minutes, until puffy and golden, rotating the pans halfway through. Remove from the oven and serve immediately, or leave in the oven, turn the oven off, and open the door slightly to keep the puffs warm for up to 1 hour.

Makes about 3 dozen puffs

ESCAROLE SALAD WITH
ANCHOVY-GARLIC DRESSING

A can of anchovies in olive oil, which costs about a dollar, can revolutionize a salad. This escarole salad yields a bonus, a mountain of discarded dark outer leaves, which can be braised like chard or layered into lasagna.

2 to 3 heads escarole, pale green
  and yellow inner leaves only
8 anchovy fillets, drained and
  coarsely chopped
4 large garlic cloves, minced

2½ tablespoons fresh lemon juice
½ cup extra-virgin olive oil
Kosher salt and freshly ground
  black pepper

Separate the escarole leaves, wash very well, and dry. Keep refrigerated until ready to serve: the leaves should be cool when served.

Mash the anchovies, garlic, and lemon juice in a small bowl. Drizzle in the olive oil, whisking furiously. Add salt to taste and plenty of black pepper.

Toss the escarole with about half the dressing, then add more to taste, tossing gently but with determination to coat every leaf. Serve.

Makes 6 to 8 servings

PASTA WITH ROAST CHICKEN, CURRANTS, AND PINE NUTS

Using a whole chicken and its golden fat to sauce a pound and a half of pasta—what could be more economical than that? The only improvement I have made on this traditional Jewish-Italian recipe, which comes from Venice via the cookbook writer Claudia Roden, is to use thighs instead of a whole bird: more meat, more fat, less money. Dried rosemary is a frugal, almost unnoticeable substitute for fresh.

3½ pounds bone-in, skin-on chicken thighs, patted dry

Salt and freshly ground black pepper

Paprika

3 tablespoons unsalted butter, cut into pieces

1½ pounds bucatini or linguine

2 teaspoons crumbled dried rosemary

½ cup dried currants or raisins

⅔ cup pine nuts, toasted until golden in a skillet or 250-degree oven

3 tablespoons chopped fresh parsley

Preheat the oven to 375 degrees (if the oven has a convection feature, use it).

Arrange the thighs in a large roasting pan, preferably nonstick. Sprinkle generously with salt, pepper, and paprika and dot with the butter. Bake for about 35 minutes, until the thighs are just cooked through and the skin is crisp.

Meanwhile, bring a large pot of salted water to a boil.

When the chicken is done, let cool slightly, then use your hands (rubber gloves are helpful) to pull the meat and skin from the bones, making bite-sized pieces. Reserve the meat and skin in the roasting pan; discard the bones.

Meanwhile, add the pasta to the boiling water and cook just until tender.

Reserving 1 cup of the cooking water, drain the pasta and add to the roasting pan. Add ½ cup of the pasta water to the roasting pan and set over low heat. Add the rosemary, currants, and pine nuts and toss, then add more salt and pepper to taste, and more cooking water if the mixture seems dry. Sprinkle with the parsley and serve immediately in shallow bowls.

Makes 6 servings

TANGERINE-VANILLA FLOATS

It's always more cost-effective to splurge on the produce than on the protein. A dozen top-quality tangerines in season cost me only $3; a top-quality roast of beef would cost twenty times that. Fresh orange juice can be used instead of tangerine juice, but it should be very sweet and not too acidic; add superfine sugar to taste if necessary.

This recipe, modest as it is, was the inspiration of California chef Suzanne Goin, who has magical abilities with citrus.

6 large scoops vanilla ice cream   Seltzer
3 cups fresh tangerine juice (from
    about 12 tangerines)

Divide the ice cream among six medium glasses or cups. Add ½ cup tangerine juice to each cup and top off with seltzer. Serve with straws and spoons.

Makes 6 servings

FEBRUARY

THE COMFORT CHALLENGE

THE COMFORT CHALLENGE

by **JULIA MOSKIN**

Comfort food was not something I understood the need for until about my thirty-fifth birthday. Until then, breakups and hurt feelings were the extent of my personal heartaches. The only death I had witnessed was that of Murphy, my childhood pet (and a wonderful cat she was too). Nothing happened that a big bag of Nacho Cheese Doritos couldn't cure.

Of course, such privilege couldn't last. If your friends are as close as family, like mine, and if your family is tight and loving, like mine, you learn a lot about helplessness and failure later on. You can't protect your sister from having her heart broken, or your parents from getting older, or your kids from being terrorized by crazies yelling on the street. (I live across the street from a public park that is popular with actors, dogs, and lunatics.) You can't protect yourself from stress and sadness.

Severson is way ahead of me when it comes to heartache—hey, no fair! She was living hard when I was still going around in pink leg warmers. She moved and changed schools often as a child. She had to come out as a lesbian to a Catholic mother and Norwegian father. She had to find the strength to stop drinking, forever, an epic act of self-control that I admire her for every day. When it comes to needing and providing comfort, she had a major head start. And, to her credit, she doesn't hold that against me. Much.

By now, we have both learned the same truth: there isn't much you can do for people mired in trouble or tragedy except show up, preferably with food. Showing up is never the wrong thing to do. And there are many occasions in life when a casserole is more eloquent than a card.

But what kind? Homemade goes without saying. Think big, and kid-friendly, and easy to heat up. You can't invite your sad pal over for takeout. Don't send a fruit basket or even cookies from Williams-Sonoma (no matter how fancy the cookies are). All these things are nice to receive, but not what you really want to eat when you are sad. In my opinion, only the cheesiest of the cheesy, only the most buttery and savory and spoonable of foods are right for hard times.

The small humiliations of daily life demand comfort too.

The first time I ever felt like a worm in the kitchen was at the James Beard House in Greenwich Village. I was filling in as a kitchen assistant for a vegetarian chef who was floundering through a book tour. She had brought twenty pounds of precious marble-sized potatoes from her own garden in Virginia, and she thrust them at me and said, "Parcook these," before rushing off again. I don't remember exactly what I did except to rig up a vast steamer that warmed the potatoes slightly without cooking them at all. I do remember the embarrassment I felt that kept me from asking, "How?" as well as the humiliation when she came back an hour later, shot me a withering look, and ejected me from the kitchen. I went straight home, stopping only for Doritos and white wine, and woke up the next morning with a bed full of crumbs and a killer headache.

A little courage would have saved me that humiliation. Cooking is not hard. As with driving or Tweeting, millions of perfect idiots do it every day.

Since then, I've cooked with all kinds of chefs and learned that they ask how as often as toddlers do. There are as many ways to chop an onion or boil an egg as there are flowers in the meadow. Asking how, like bringing food to those who need comfort, is always the right thing to do.

BLACK BEAN SOUP WITH PINK PICKLED ONIONS

This was my first attempt at Soup for the Sad. The people I made it for—whom I barely knew, but whose baby daughter was undergoing heart surgery—still talk about it. (She is about to graduate from high school.) And considering that the soup takes all of about thirty minutes to put together, a fifteen-year deposit into the bank of human goodwill was a remarkable return on investment. I also brought them a bottle of te-quila, which goes well with the green fire of the chiles.

Unlike many black bean soups, this one is minimally seasoned—no cumin, no chipotle—which makes it more surprising that the recipe was developed long ago by my friend Bobby Flay. When I was a baby food writer and he was a bad-boy chef in the East Village, I went to his restaurant, Miracle Grill, often. This soup brings back those crazy nights of the early 1990s, when squeeze bottles and prickly pear margaritas seemed like the coolest ideas ever.

FOR THE ONIONS
2 red onions, thinly sliced

1 cup cider vinegar

1 teaspoon salt

FOR THE SOUP
2 tablespoons olive oil

1 medium carrot, peeled and coarsely chopped

1 medium Spanish onion, coarsely chopped

3 garlic cloves, coarsely chopped

1 cup red wine

Three 15-ounce cans black beans, drained and rinsed

3 jalapeños, roasted, peeled, and seeded

1 poblano chile, roasted, peeled, and seeded (optional)

4 cups water

2 tablespoons fresh lime juice

Salt and freshly ground black pepper

Optional garnishes: toasted cumin seeds, fresh cilantro leaves, and/or sour cream or Greek yogurt

To make the onions: Bring a pot of water to a boil. Add the onions and blanch for 1 minute, then drain in a colander. Return the onions to the pot and add the cider vinegar, salt, and just enough cold water to barely cover the onions. Bring to a boil over high heat, reduce the heat, and simmer for 1 minute. Transfer the onions and brine to a glass jar and let cool, then seal the jar. (The onions can be refrigerated indefinitely.)

To make the soup: Heat the oil in a large saucepan over medium heat. Add the carrot, onion, and garlic and cook until the onion is translucent, about 5 minutes. Add the wine, bring to a boil, and cook until the liquid is reduced by half.

Add the beans, chiles, and water, bring to a simmer, and simmer for 30 minutes.

Using a blender or food processor, puree half of the soup, and return it to the pan. Add the lime juice and salt and pepper to taste.

Serve hot, topped with the pickled onions and the garnishes of your choice.

Makes 8 to 10 servings

CHEESE GRITS WITH SCALLIONS, BACON, AND RED PEPPER

Shrimp and grits without the shrimp, this dish fits neatly into the modern comfort zone. It is rich, soft, savory, and easy, and—very important—it can be made with things I have hanging around in the refrigerator at all times. Shrimp are all very well, but they are a pain to deal with.

It is perfectly fine if your scallions are a bit exhausted and the bell pepper heading toward its end. Everything cooks together into a savory mass that shows off the creamy grits and their bright corn flavor. Leftovers make a fantastic breakfast with fried eggs.

2 cups milk
5 cups water
½ teaspoon salt, plus more
   to taste
2 cups yellow corn grits,
   preferably coarse-ground
8 ounces thick-cut bacon
1 red bell pepper, cored, seeded, and finely
   diced
½ cup finely chopped scallions
1 teaspoon all-purpose flour
2 cups coarsely grated cheddar cheese
   (about 8 ounces)
Freshly ground black pepper
  Cold unsalted butter to taste

Combine the milk, 4 cups of the water, and the salt in a medium pot and heat to a simmer. Whisk in the grits, reduce the heat, cover, and simmer, stirring occasionally, until the grits are creamy and soft, about 15 minutes.

Meanwhile, slowly cook the bacon in a wide skillet over low heat until it is crisp and has rendered its fat. Do not let the fat scorch; you need it for the gravy. Drain the bacon on paper towels and pour off all but 3 tablespoons of the fat from the skillet. Cut or crumble the bacon into pieces.

Reheat the skillet over medium heat. Add the red pepper and most of the scallions and cook, stirring, until they are very soft and the edges are golden, 8 to 10 minutes. Sprinkle the flour over and cook, stirring, until golden, 1 to 2 minutes. Add the remaining 1 cup water and cook until thickened.

Just before serving, mix the cheese and a few teaspoons of cold butter into the grits. Taste and add more salt, some freshly ground pepper, and/or butter as needed. Serve in bowls, topped with the scallion–red pepper gravy, bacon bits, and the remaining chopped scallion.

Makes 6 to 8 servings

CRUSTY MACARONI AND CHEESE

In 2004, when the *New York Times* website began tracking the most e-mailed stories of the day, the competitive air of the newsroom—already scary to a newcomer like me—became almost unbreathable. It was exciting for us writers, who had never had any way of knowing which stories were actually read, to see the results. Stories about pets, yoga, and Alzheimer's disease often seemed to be at the top, but that didn't stop a girl from dreaming.

And then, at the gray tail end of 2005, after the holiday-cooking Armageddon had blown through the Dining section and we were all running on fumes, I was assigned to come up with a cover story—something, anything—for the first Wednesday of the new year. The resulting article about macaroni and cheese rose to the top of the most e-mailed list and stayed there, amazingly, for months. And this recipe, simple as it is, remains the most e-mailed in *Times* history. Because of the high cheese content, one reviewer called it "Julia Moskin's disgusting macaroni and cheese recipe." I beg to differ. It's the perfect macaroni and cheese recipe.

3 tablespoons unsalted butter	1 pound elbow pasta
12 ounces extra-sharp cheddar cheese, coarsely grated	⅛ teaspoon cayenne pepper (optional)
12 ounces American or cheddar cheese, coarsely grated	Salt
	⅔ cup whole milk

Preheat the oven to 375 degrees. Use 1 tablespoon of the butter to thickly grease a 9-by-13-inch baking dish.

Combine the grated cheeses; set aside 2 heaping cups for the topping.

Boil the pasta in salted water until just tender, drain, and rinse under cold water.

Toss together the pasta, the remaining cheese, the cayenne, if using, and salt to taste in a large bowl. Put in the prepared baking dish and pour the milk evenly over the surface. Sprinkle the reserved cheese on top and dot with the remaining 2 tablespoons butter.

Bake, uncovered, for 45 minutes. Raise the heat to 400 degrees and bake for 15 to 20 minutes more, until crusty on the top and bottom.

Makes one 9-by-13-inch baking dish, about 8 servings

BOEUF BOURGUIGNON WITH
CHIVE MASHED POTATOES

One of the first meals that Kim and I ever cooked together included pommes Chantilly, mashed potatoes covered in oven-glazed whipped cream, which sounded irresistible to both of us. For some reason, we decided it would be spectacular fun to shape the tall pile of potatoes into a pyramid. We did not notice that as we patted it down, the fluffy mound was compressed into a hard, airless mass. When the demented thing came out of the oven, with flaming whipped cream sliding down its sides (and onto the oven floor), we were forced to admit defeat. Lesson learned: some things are better not messed with.

For this rib-sticking combination of beef and potatoes, life's usual cooking patterns are reversed. The meat takes almost no prep time at all, asking only to be allowed to simmer for a while, then set aside to collect its flavors. It is a French housewife's recipe, not the fancy version with those annoying pearl onions. But the mashed potatoes are coddled into the oven and generally treated like a precious elixir. The recipe comes from a chef in Maine, where potatoes are taken very seriously. Glazing the tops of the potato-filled ramekins with more butter is the kind of nice touch that makes people feel comforted and taken care of, but it is not strictly necessary.

FOR THE STEW

1 tablespoon vegetable oil

3 ounces onions or shallots, chopped

3½ ounces thick-cut bacon, diced

1½ pounds stewing beef, cut into 1½-inch pieces, and patted dry

Scant ¼ cup all-purpose flour

1¼ cups stock (any type), hot

1¼ cups red wine

1 bouquet garni (1 bay leaf, 3 fresh thyme sprigs, and 3 fresh parsley sprigs, tied together with kitchen twine)

Freshly ground black pepper

3½ ounces mushrooms, chopped

Salt

FOR THE MASH

2 pounds waxy potatoes, such as Yukon Gold, peeled

1 pound russet (baking) potatoes

12 garlic cloves, lightly crushed and peeled

1 cup buttermilk

¼ cup heavy cream

Salt and freshly ground black
  pepper

8 tablespoons (1 stick) unsalted
  butter, melted

¼ cup chopped fresh chives

To make the stew: Heat the oil in a heavy pot over medium heat. Add the onions and bacon and cook, stirring, until browned. Remove them with a slotted spoon, leaving the fat in the pot, and set aside.

Add the beef to the pot and brown on all sides (work in 2 batches if needed to avoid crowding, then return all the beef to the pot).

Sprinkle the browned beef with the flour, stirring until the flour has browned, then add the hot stock. Stir, scraping the bottom of the pot, then add the bacon and onions, wine, and bouquet garni, season with pepper, and bring to a simmer. Simmer very gently for 2 hours.

Add the mushrooms to the stew and cook for 30 minutes more. Season with salt and serve. (Or, even better, make the stew ahead, then reheat and serve the next day.)

Meanwhile, make the potatoes: Put the potatoes and garlic cloves in a large pot of cold salted water, bring to a boil, and boil gently over medium heat until tender, about 40 minutes. Scoop out and set aside ½ cup of the cooking water, then drain the potatoes and garlic in a colander.

Preheat the oven to 425 degrees.

Bring the buttermilk and heavy cream to a simmer in a saucepan over medium heat (the mixture will look curdled). Remove from the heat.

Put the potatoes and garlic in a large pot and set over medium-low heat. Pour in about three-quarters of the hot buttermilk mixture and coarsely mash with a potato masher. Season with salt and pepper. Check the texture: if needed, thin the mixture with the remaining hot buttermilk and reserved cooking water. Stir in 6 tablespoons of the butter and the chives.

Divide the mashed potatoes among six to eight ramekins or transfer to a large baking dish. Drizzle with the remaining butter. Transfer to the oven and bake for about 20 minutes, until lightly browned.

Ladle the stew into bowls and serve with the potatoes.

Makes 6 to 8 servings

STICKY TOFFEE PUDDING

When I first tasted this bittersweet, caramel-laden cake at an English tea shop, I thought it was far too tasty to be British. I am still suspicious, because although I love British desserts, they don't usually have the edge that makes this one irresistible—plus, the dates seem so American (see Kim's Date-Nut Bread, page 227, a pale imitation of this cake IMHO). Because of the baking soda's effect, the dates truly disappear into the batter, so even if you don't particularly like dates, you'll find the cake exquisitely dark and lush. The contrasts of texture and temperature are totally seductive.

It may be a bit much for an after-dinner treat, but when you need dessert to be the entire meal—and this has happened to me with unnerving frequency in recent years—sticky toffee pudding is just the ticket.

FOR THE CAKE
12 ounces dates, pitted and
    roughly chopped
2½ cups water
2 teaspoons baking soda
3¼ cups sifted all-purpose flour
2 teaspoons baking powder
8 tablespoons (1 stick) unsalted
    butter, cut into pieces, at room
    temperature
1⅔ cups granulated sugar
4 large eggs
2 teaspoons vanilla extract

FOR THE SAUCE
2¼ cups packed light brown sugar
7 tablespoons unsalted butter
1 cup half-and-half

1 teaspoon brandy
¼ teaspoon vanilla extract
1 cup very cold heavy cream

To make the cake: Preheat the oven to 350 degrees. Line a 9-by-13-inch baking pan with parchment or waxed paper.

Combine the dates and water in a saucepan and bring to a boil. Remove from the heat and gradually stir in the baking soda (it will foam up). Set aside.

Combine the flour and baking powder in a bowl.

In the bowl of a stand mixer fitted with the paddle attachment, cream the butter until fluffy. Add the sugar and cream until fluffy. Without stopping the mixer, add 2 of the eggs and mix until combined. Add the remaining 2 eggs and vanilla and mix until combined. Add about one-third of the flour mixture and one-third of the dates, with their liquid, and mix until combined. Add the remaining flour and date mixtures in 2 additions each, mixing until incorporated.

Pour the batter into the prepared baking pan and bake for about 40 minutes, until firm and set in the center. Let cool completely in the pan, then turn out of the pan onto a baking sheet and peel off the paper. (The cake can be made up to 2 days in advance. Wrap in plastic wrap and refrigerate. Set on a baking sheet and bring to room temperature before proceeding.)

When ready to serve, preheat the oven to 400 degrees.

To make the sauce: Combine the brown sugar, butter, half-and-half, and brandy in a saucepan, bring to a boil, and boil for 3 minutes. Remove from the heat and stir in the vanilla.

Pour the sauce evenly over the top of the cake. Bake for about 5 minutes, until the sauce is bubbly and the cake is heated through.

Meanwhile, whip the heavy cream to soft peaks.

Cut the cake into squares and serve hot, with the cold whipped cream.

Makes one 9-by-13-inch cake

FEBRUARY

THE COMFORT CHALLENGE

---

by **KIM SEVERSON**

Things happen in life. Bad things. Sad things. Things that just aren't right or fair or kind.

For me, the solution is food. For Julia too. It's at the heart of why we're such dear friends.

People who know us might guess that in times of crisis, I would be the one most likely to reach for the messier indulgences—the carb-loaded joys of a big bowl of creamy pasta or the sweet buzzy release from a big piece of something chocolate. After all, Julia's the one with the yoga body, and tasteful wardrobe, and pristine house (no untidy stacks of papers and tattered kids' toys there!).

They might even think I'd be the one most likely to uncork a bottle of red and get down to the business of forgetting whatever it is that sucked. And that was, for many years, true. I spent a good part of my adulthood drinking away the pain of bad days. I sought peace as well in calories and fat. But those days are behind me. (OK, maybe not the part about the fat, but still. . . .)

When I stopped drinking several years ago, a surprising thing happened. Food became more important. I saw how food was history and solace and hope, how it made an instant community of the people who shared it. And it was especially nice that I was a better cook sober than drunk. I saw that clean is the better path.

So now when someone shows up on my doorstep newly heartbroken, grieving over an aging parent or just worn out from the day, I look to put something more restorative and light on the table.

The path out of whatever pain my friend has brought to the table begins with a bracing cocktail without alcohol. Pink peppercorns offer heat, and thyme, depth. It will wake up the senses.

Next I'll set out a little plate of homemade sesame wafers. My dear Leslie taught me a good recipe for what Southerners call benne seed wafers. The benne seed—its name is derived from the Nigerian word for sesame seed—is a nod to the African roots of much of Southern cooking. The little seeds are supposed to bring good luck, which anyone can appreciate, whether life is in the weeds or not.

The recipe is very forgiving. The dough can be made ahead of time and held in the refrigerator, so you can take as much as you need, roll it out, cut the crackers, and bake them quickly. Or cook the whole batch ahead of time and store them in a covered container, ready for a gentle reheating. They're just fine at room temperature too.

Southerners like to top the wafers with shrimp paste, but an easier appetizer can be made by adding a smear of goat cheese into which you've mixed some crumbled nori and a touch—just a touch—of Sriracha chile sauce.

The real healer, though, is the steaming bowl of pho. I had eaten a lot of it in America before I traveled to Vietnam, but I'd never really understood the soup's power until I went there. One morning, feeling homesick and out of place, I paid a street vendor the equivalent of a dime and sat down at a rickety little metal table. He handed me a bowl of beef broth and noodles, pho so fragrant and light that I immediately felt at one with the place and, most important, myself.

Give your sad guest the same experience.

A side plate of fresh herbs like basil and some crunchy bean sprouts should be at the ready, giving the heartbroken something to occupy her mind and her hands. Working the soft, thin noodles into her mouth with a spoon and chopsticks will remind her that she can take care of herself. The warm taste of bone marrow and star anise will fortify her weary soul.

Then put away the tissues, go for a few good laughs, and offer your friend—or your sad self—the comfort of a soft, smooth panna cotta made with ginger-infused cream that has also been flavored with cornflakes.

Tomorrow, after all, is another day.

PINK PEPPERCORN COCKTAILS

This has a complex-tasting simple syrup as its base, and a refreshing note of lime and mint. One could certainly add vodka to make it a more traditional cocktail.

1 cup sugar

1 cup water

1 cinnamon stick

1 tablespoon lightly crushed
   black peppercorns

2 tablespoons lightly crushed
   pink peppercorns

A fresh thyme sprig

Several sprigs of fresh mint

2 limes, halved

Seltzer

Combine the sugar, water, cinnamon stick, peppercorns, and thyme in a saucepan and bring to a simmer, stirring to dissolve the sugar. Simmer for about 10 minutes, then remove from the heat and let stand for 3 hours. Strain. The simple syrup can be made ahead and chilled.

To serve, crush several mint leaves in the bottom of each glass. Add ¼ cup of the syrup and the juice of half a lime to each one and fill with ice. Top off with seltzer, stir well, and serve.

Makes 4 servings

HOMEMADE SESAME CRACKERS WITH SPICY NORI–GOAT CHEESE SPREAD

These crackers can take a lot of toppings. The creaminess of goat cheese, seasoned with almost anything, works well with their hearty, savory taste. You can add fresh herbs and scallions, or lemon zest and thyme, even capers and a bit of smoked salmon or baked shrimp blended together in a food processor. In the South, the crackers are sometimes made sweet with brown sugar. This version will keep for about a week in an airtight container.

FOR THE CRACKERS

1 cup sesame seeds
3 cups all-purpose flour
1½ teaspoons baking powder
1 teaspoon kosher salt, plus more for sprinkling
⅔ cup lard (try to get good-quality lard, but you can use vegetable shortening in a pinch)
⅔ cup milk

FOR THE TOPPING

1 large sheet nori, toasted in a dry sauté pan for about 30 seconds on each side
1 cup soft goat cheese or fresh ricotta
2 teaspoons Sriracha or other chile sauce

To make the crackers: Preheat the oven to 425 degrees.

Gently toast the sesame seeds in a sauté pan until they are a rich golden color and smell roasted. Be careful—they can burn in a second. Cool on a plate.

Whisk the flour, baking powder, and salt together in a large bowl. Cut in the lard as you would for piecrust, using your fingers to break up the pieces of lard and coat them with flour. The mixture should resemble coarse sand. Stir in the sesame seeds and milk and mix until blended.

Gather up the dough and turn it out onto a floured surface. Roll it out as thin as a dime. (You can do this in 2 batches.) Prick the dough with a fork at regular intervals, then cut into rounds with a 2-inch cookie cutter and arrange on an ungreased baking sheet. You can reroll the scraps of dough and stamp out more wafers.

Bake for 12 to 14 minutes, until the wafers are golden brown. Remove from the oven and sprinkle the tops with salt. Transfer to a rack to cool, and repeat until all the dough is used.

To make the topping: Crush the nori into the goat cheese. Add the Sriracha and mix well. Let sit for at least 10 minutes. (The topping makes enough for about 3 dozen wafers.)

Spread the cheese on the crackers to serve, or let guests help themselves to it from a bowl.

Makes 4 to 5 dozen crackers

PHO

This is an amalgam of recipes, and I've found that it's a very forgiving soup. It does take patience to find the right kind of bones and to simmer and strain the broth. Be gentle when you cook the broth to avoid making the soup cloudy. You can mix up the meats, or even make little lemongrass-scented meatballs or use tendon, which is common in Vietnam. Put a bottle of Sriracha and a bowl of hoisin on the table when you serve it.

FOR THE BROTH

6 pounds good beef bones, such as shank (have the butcher saw them lengthwise if they are very big; or mix in shank bones cut for osso buco or soup)

1 pound beef chuck, boneless (or similar beef; stew meat works too)

6 quarts water

2 onions, cut in half

5-inch piece of ginger, peeled

2 tablespoons vegetable oil

1 cinnamon stick

5 star anise

1 tablespoon coriander seeds

1 tablespoon fennel seeds

2 cardamom pods

8 cloves

1½ tablespoons salt, plus more to taste

1 tablespoon sugar

¼ cup fish sauce

12 ounces flank steak or round
   steak
1 bunch each fresh mint, basil,
   and cilantro
3 limes, quartered

2 jalapeños, sliced
8 ounces bean sprouts
2 pounds dried rice noodles
Hoisin sauce
Sriracha sauce

To make the broth: Put the bones in a very large pot and add water to cover. Bring to a boil and boil for 10 minutes. Drain, rinse the pot, and add the 6 quarts water, parboiled bones, and the chuck. Bring to a boil, then lower the heat and simmer, removing the scum that rises.

Meanwhile, preheat the broiler. Put the onion and ginger on a pan and rub with the oil. Broil for about 5 minutes, until charred on one side. Turn and char the other side.

Place the spices on a piece of cheesecloth and tie into a bundle with kitchen string. Add to the pot, along with the onion, ginger, salt, sugar, and fish sauce. Simmer for about 1½ hours, skimming off any scum that forms on the surface. Remove the meat and reserve. Strain the broth, clean the pot, and return the broth to the pot. Taste and adjust for seasoning with salt.

Meanwhile, put the flank steak in the freezer for about 15 minutes, then slice it thin against the grain. The steak will get cooked by the hot broth. Shred the cooked meat. Arrange the herbs, limes, jalapeños, and bean sprouts on a platter.

When ready to serve, bring the broth to a boil. Plunge the noodles into a pan of boiling water for 5 to 10 seconds to soften; drain.

Place a mound of noodles in each bowl, add some broth, and arrange a serving of the meats on top. Serve with hoisin and Sriracha on the table.

Guests can select a variety of accompaniments and sauces to dress their soup.

Makes 6 to 8 servings

CEREAL-MILK AND
GINGER PANNA COTTA

The idea for using cereal to flavor milk for desserts comes from Christina Tosi, the fine pastry chef of the Momofuku empire in New York. The trick to this dish is a good steeping of the milk. To peel the ginger, use the tip of a teaspoon to scrape away the skin.

4 cups cornflakes

2 cups heavy cream

1½ cups half-and-half

1 teaspoon salt

½ cup sugar

1 teaspoon vanilla extract

1 tablespoon grated peeled
   fresh ginger

1 envelope flavorless gelatin

4 teaspoons water

Preheat the oven to 325 degrees.

Put the cornflakes in a shallow baking pan and toast in the oven for about 10 minutes, until they start to smell toasty and turn a deeper golden.

Put the cornflakes in a large bowl and cover with the cream and half-and-half, stirring until all the flakes are wet. Steep for 30 minutes.

Strain the cream through a sieve, pushing out as much liquid as possible with a wooden spoon into a saucepan. Add the salt, sugar, vanilla, and ginger to the saucepan and heat gently to a simmer, then turn off the heat and let sit for 20 minutes.

Put the gelatin in a medium bowl, add the water, and stir to dissolve. Add the cream mixture and whisk to combine.

Using a very light hand, oil the inside of six small ramekins or silicone molds. Divide the cream mixture among them, cover with plastic wrap, and chill until set. To serve, invert each panna cotta onto a plate and gently pull off the ramekin or mold, shaking the panna cotta onto the plate.

Makes 6 servings

MARCH
THE CHILDREN'S CHALLENGE

THE CHILDREN'S CHALLENGE

by **KIM SEVERSON**

Julia had children before I did. Like so many things in our relationship, this gave her an edge. A little sliver of superiority. (I am sure that by this point you have figured out that this is a trait I love about Julia. In no way do I mind that she makes me feel inferior in many areas of life. I welcome it—in the way a schoolboy appreciates a paddle to the ass.)

But I digress. What I want to talk about is our children's challenge—that is, how to cook to best celebrate a child's birthday.

Now, to be fair, Julia has provided many firsts for my daughter, Sammy. We had her first Passover at Julia's house, with all the fancy china and homemade matzo balls. Julia gave us a smart book about donut makers, which my kid cherishes and expensive French baby clothes as hand-me-downs.

You would think, with all that fanciness, that Julia might also take the fancy road when it comes to a children's birthday party. But no. She's all baked potato bars and Devil Dog cake.

So this is where I knew I would best her. The challenge of a great children's party, I think, is to make food sophisticated enough for the adults but fun enough for the children and generally delicious enough so everyone eats and is happy.

Enter the salad in a cup, a simple trick that appeals to both grown-ups and kids.

The idea is to toss sturdy romaine leaves in a light Caesar-style dressing (coddle the eggs so they aren't raw, for the children's sake) and arrange three or four leaves, along with a crouton stick, in each plastic cup.

Fill out the rest of the menu with little cups of bean soup, tiny biscuits spread with butter and jam or ham, and cucumber tea sandwiches.

Although the cucumber sandwiches are simple, they do rely on a couple of key techniques. Because there are so few ingredients—cucumbers, butter, and white bread—everything needs to be just right. Very fresh English cucumbers or small Persians work best. You don't want a seedy cucumber. They must be sliced so thin that one needs a few layers to make the filling substantial enough. And the butter should be salted. Sweet butter doesn't have enough flavor. Spread it when it's at room temperature but not too soft.

And the bread. Thin white sandwich bread works best and offers a good compromise between convenience and flavor. Buy a Pullman loaf and have it sliced thin—give yourself a break. You have a cake to make!

I am in love with layer cakes. Ever since I headed south to learn about the art of Southern layer cakes, I have been convinced that no one else does it better. These women do twelve or thirteen layers sometimes, baking them three at

a time in cake pans. I opt for three layers, which I think is still spectacular and not too insane.

Instead of a sugary cake or devil's food or the punitive kid's birthday cake for the health set, carrot cake, I went for a Southern classic that will appeal to both adults and kids (who I might point out, will actually eat real food). It's called a lemon cheese layer cake, but it has nothing to do with cheese or cheesecake. The "cheese" is a lemon curd that fills and frosts a white cake. In this recipe, the curd is simmered, like a custard filling. I have seen recipes that allow you to make the lemon curd in a microwave, and that works pretty well, but there is silkiness to the curd done this way. And since the recipe is adapted from Chef Scott Peacock, I would not dare to compromise.

The children deserve it. And so do I.

HAM BISCUITS, JAM BISCUITS

These little biscuits, an adaptation of recipes from a couple of my favorite Southern chefs, should be made the day of the party. The trick is to use a sharp cutter and to push down firmly, never twisting, when you cut them. Purists like lard, but butter, or even shortening, will work. You may have a lot of little trimmings—bake them too and use them as a diversion when people come into the kitchen looking to snag one of the real biscuits.

FOR THE BISCUITS
5 cups sifted unbleached all-purpose flour
1½ tablespoons baking powder
1 tablespoon kosher salt
½ cup packed lard or 8 tablespoons
   (1 stick) unsalted butter, chilled and
   cut into pieces
2 cups chilled buttermilk, or as needed

⅓ cup (10⅔ tablespoons) butter, at
   room temperature
8 thin slices good ham, cut into small
   squares
2 or 3 sour dill pickles or several
   cornichons, thinly sliced
¼ cup jam, homemade (see page 53)
   or store-bought

To make the biscuits: Position a rack in the upper third of the oven and preheat the oven to 500 degrees. Line a heavy baking sheet with parchment paper.

Whisk together the flour, baking powder, and salt in a large bowl. Add the lard, coating it in flour. Working quickly, rub the fat between your fingertips until roughly half is coarse and half remains in large pieces, about ¾ inch.

Make a well in the center of the flour mixture. Add the buttermilk all at once and, with a large spoon, stir quickly just until the mixture is blended and begins to form a sticky dough (if the dough appears dry, add 1 to 2 tablespoons additional buttermilk). Don't overwork the dough.

Turn the dough out onto a generously floured surface. Using floured hands, knead 8 to 10 times, until a cohesive ball of dough forms. Gently flatten the dough to an even thickness. Using a floured rolling pin, lightly roll out the dough to a ¾-inch thickness (the shape doesn't matter). Using a dinner fork dipped in flour, pierce the dough completely through at ½-inch intervals to give the biscuits lift. Flour a small biscuit cutter, about 1½ inches in diameter, and cut out biscuits, getting as close to the previous cut as you can each time. Arrange on the parchment-lined baking sheet.

Bake for 6 to 10 minutes, until the tops are golden brown. Remove from the oven and let cool on a rack.

With a delicate hand and a serrated knife, slice the biscuits open. Spread the bottoms and tops with the softened butter. Add a couple of small slices of ham and a slice of pickle to half the bottoms and a good smear of jam to the rest. Replace the tops and serve.

Makes about 30 little biscuits

Quick Jam with Frozen Strawberries

Some smart chefs have taught me that sometimes the simplest things can be the best. Like this jam. Enlist your child to help make it. Kids can measure sugar or strawberries and help squeeze juice from the lemon.

4 cups unsweetened frozen strawberries	2 cups sugar Juice of 1 lemon

Put the berries in a large bowl with the sugar and let them defrost and get juicy.

Put the berry mixture in a pot and bring to a boil. Lower the heat to a strong simmer and add the lemon juice. Attach a candy thermometer to the pot and cook until the mixture reaches 225 degrees, about 30 minutes. Let cool, then pour into a glass jar and refrigerate, for up to 1 month.

Makes about 5 cups

CAESAR SALAD IN A CUP

This is the best party food, and easier than ever with precleaned romaine lettuce that comes in a bag. The dressing is adapted from the one Julia Child developed after recalling a childhood memory in which she saw Caesar Cardini make his salad in Tijuana, Mexico, and later interviewed his daughter. For people worried about salmonella from eggs, this method of coddling will make them safe but keep the eggs very runny, which is important for the dressing. Use festive plastic cups for serving, and encourage guests to eat the leaves with their fingers.

5 romaine lettuce hearts
1 loaf French or other white bread
   (unsliced)
3 large garlic cloves
Salt
¾ cup extra-virgin olive oil, or
   more as needed

2 large eggs
Freshly ground black pepper
Juice of 1½ large lemons, or more
   to taste
6 drops Worcestershire sauce
½ cup freshly grated Parmesan
   cheese

Wash and shake excess water from the romaine. Shake excess water from romaine. Separate the leaves and lay them on a couple of large clean kitchen towels.

Roll up gently to dry. (This step can be done ahead of time; store the whole roll in the refrigerator.)

Preheat the oven to 350 degrees.

Slice the loaf lengthwise into planks, then slice each plank into breadsticks, 6 or 7 inches long.

Mince and mash the garlic with ¼ teaspoon salt, then mix with ¼ cup of the oil. Pour into a large baking pan, add the sticks, and toss to coat. Spread the sticks out and bake for 12 to 15 minutes, turning occasionally, until crispy. Let cool.

Pierce the large ends of the eggs with an egg pricker or tack and lower them into a saucepan of boiling water. Boil for about 1 minute; remove and set aside to cool. (The eggs can be put in the refrigerator until it's time to assemble the salad.)

Saving the smaller leaves for another use, put the lettuce leaves in a large roasting pan or other good-sized vessel. Pour the remaining ½ cup of oil over the romaine and toss to coat the leaves. Sprinkle on ⅓ teaspoon salt and several grinds of pepper and toss again. Drizzle with the lemon juice and sprinkle with the Worcestershire. Break in the eggs and toss to blend. Taste a leaf and correct the seasoning if necessary, adding a bit more oil or lemon. Quickly toss with the cheese.

Stand 3 or 4 leaves in each cup, stick in a crouton, and serve.

Makes 18 servings

WHITE BEAN SOUP WITH CHIVE OIL

This creamy soup, served in tiny cups and bright with chive oil, is easy to make and serve. Kids will like the little cups and the crazy green swirl. Adults will appreciate the healthfulness and the flavor.

2 cups dried Great Northern or
   other small white beans, rinsed
   and picked over
3 tablespoons olive oil
1 large onion, chopped
1 cup chopped leeks (white and
   pale green parts only)
1 large tomato, halved, seeded,
   and chopped
½ cup chopped carrots
½ cup chopped celery
8 garlic cloves, chopped

11 cups homemade chicken stock
   or canned low-salt chicken
   broth, or more as needed
1 tablespoon chopped fresh
   thyme
1 tablespoon chopped fresh
   rosemary
½ cup half-and-half
Salt and freshly ground black
   pepper
Chive Oil for drizzling (recipe
   follows)

Put the beans in a large pot, add enough water to cover the beans by 2 inches, and let soak overnight. Drain.

Heat the olive oil in the same pot over medium-high heat. Add the onion, leeks, tomato, carrots, celery, and garlic and sauté until tender, about 6 minutes. Add the beans, chicken stock, thyme, and rosemary and bring to a boil. Reduce the heat to medium-low, cover, and simmer, stirring occasionally, until the beans are very tender, about 1 hour.

Working in batches, puree the soup in a blender until smooth. Return the soup to the pot and add the half-and-half, then add more chicken stock to thin the soup if needed, and reheat the soup if necessary. Season to taste with salt and pepper.

Ladle into espresso cups and top each with a few squirts or a drizzle of chive oil.

Makes 18 small servings

Chive Oil

1 bunch fresh chives
½ cup canola oil
⅛ teaspoon sea salt

Freshly ground black pepper to taste

Fill a bowl with ice cubes and water. Blanch the chives in boiling water for 30 seconds, then drain immediately and put the chives in the ice water. Drain, wrap in paper towels, and squeeze out the excess water.

Put the chives in a blender with the remaining ingredients and blend for 2 minutes; strain through a fine sieve. Transfer the oil to a plastic squeeze bottle if you like. The oil can be refrigerated for up to a month; bring to room temperature before using.

Makes ½ cup

LEMON CHEESE LAYER CAKE

This is not a cheesecake—cooks in some parts of the South have long made lemon cheese cake, a fancy cake with lemon curd for the filling and frosting. The frosting is quite translucent, acting as a glaze and a jam and icing all at once. Like most cakes, this is better with a day or two of age on it.

FOR THE CAKE

¾ pound (3 sticks) unsalted
  butter, at room temperature,
  plus more for greasing the pans
3¼ cups cake flour
2 teaspoons baking powder

¼ teaspoon salt
2 cups sugar
8 large egg whites
1 cup milk
2 teaspoons vanilla extract

FOR THE LEMON CURD

1¾ cups sugar
¾ cup fresh lemon juice
12 tablespoons (1½ sticks)
  unsalted butter, melted

8 large yolks
3 tablespoons finely grated
  lemon zest
½ teaspoon salt

To make the cake: Position a rack in the middle of the oven and preheat the oven to 350 degrees. Grease three 9-inch round cake pans and line with parchment or waxed paper.

Sift the flour, baking powder, and salt onto a piece of parchment or waxed paper.

Beat the sugar and butter in a stand mixer until light and fluffy, stopping to scrape down the sides as needed. Whisk the egg whites in a medium bowl until well blended but not foamy. Add to the batter in 4 batches, making sure each addition is well incorporated.

Add the dry ingredients and milk to the batter alternately in 4 batches, mixing only until just blended after each addition. Mix in the vanilla.

Divide the batter among the prepared pans. Gently drop each one onto the counter to eliminate large air bubbles. Bake for 20 minutes, or until a cake springs back when pressed in the center or a cake tester inserted in the center comes out clean. Let rest for 5 minutes, then remove the cake from the pans and let cool completely on a rack.

Meanwhile, make the curd: Put all the ingredients in a large nonreactive saucepan and whisk to blend. Set over medium heat, attach a candy thermometer to the saucepan, and cook, whisking constantly, until the curd thickens and the candy thermometer registers 170 degrees; this can take 10 to 15 minutes. Do not let the curd simmer or boil. Pour into a bowl and let cool to room temperature.

Place a cake layer, upside down, on a cake stand or plate and spread ⅔ cup of the curd over it to the edges. Stack another layer on top and spread with more curd, then top with the remaining layer. Spread the remaining curd over the top and sides; the layers will be visible through the curd on the sides. If the layers slide while you frost the cake, push 3 or 4 long wooden skewers through them to hold it until the curd sets, then remove them. The cake is best if left to stand, covered, at room temperature overnight.

Makes 1 large layer cake

THE CHILDREN'S CHALLENGE

by **JULIA MOSKIN**

There are two basic approaches to cooking for children. Severson, with her Norwegian backbone, belongs to the party that says that children will have to learn to eat like humans sooner or later. If they are hungry enough, they will eat.

In my experience, this is untrue. Children would much rather eat nothing than food they don't care for. And even if this is fine on paper (they won't starve), their parents will not be philosophical about their darlings' lack of food.

Severson believes that you can feed children Caesar salad at a party. This way lies madness. We ignore the tastes of children at our peril. That is how a person ends up spending her own party in the kitchen, draining some last-minute spaghetti, heating up unplanned chicken nuggets, and hating the guests.

The other position (mine, and the right one) says that childish food is one of life's great pleasures. I cook "real" food that might be intriguing to children and is delicious for adults. (Though it is always wise to order a plain pizza as backup, for there are picky people of every age in every group—why even bother cooking for them?)

After all, these parties, whatever they are celebrating, should be low pressure—no one expects the food to be sophisticated.

I like making birthday cakes; a birthday is one of the only homemade-is-

mandatory events in my culinary year. To paraphrase the writer Calvin Trillin, it is my belief that if you do not bake your child's birthday cake, the state will come and take the child. I don't know why I feel this way, but like so many things around food and family, it is both irrational and fact.

When my first child was born, I began to search for The Perfect Cake. I did not want to experiment every year. Layer cakes are not my forte ("patient" and "methodical" being words that could never be applied to me or my cooking), but I did acquire rudimentary skills in piping and swirling.

Then the pressure heightened. It turned out that modern children have not one birthday party, but several: the school party, the family fête, and the friends' soiree. And then there was another baby, with birthdays of her own. The demands for cakes multiplied. Then there was the night I stayed up until 3 a.m. fussing over a cake shaped like a train, with one cake train car for each kid in my son's preschool class (fourteen cars, including the engine: the number is seared into my brain).

It was then that I decided one homemade cake per kid per year would have to satisfy the authorities, whoever they are.

Of course, there is more to parties than cake. In my world, dinner parties have largely gone the way of the fax machine and the hair scrunchy. So I usually end up doing late-morning or afternoon gatherings that attract a multigenerational crowd.

Thinking up things that children might be excited about eating—because party food should be at least a little bit exciting—and that can also be adapted into something delicious for grown-ups occupies a great deal of my subway time. Garnishes, relishes, and dipping sauces are an excellent way of managing this. Pasta with butter for the kids; pasta with pine nuts toasted in brown butter, garnished with Parmesan shreds, for the grown-ups. Melon balls for the kids; melon balls in a fiery-sweet syrup for the adults. Plain potato chips for the kids; chips sprinkled with lemon salt for the grown-ups. These days, people are amazingly grateful even for simple treats like homemade breakfast sausage, or real whipped cream. And when in doubt, remember: everyone loves onion dip.

POTATO CHIPS
WITH LEMON SALT

This lemon salt does remarkable things to store-bought potato chips. Also to veal stew, the rim of a martini glass, roast chicken, dry-aged steak, French fish soup, and anything else you can think of.

¼ cup grated lemon zest
  (from about 3 large lemons)
¼ cup kosher salt
¼ cup flaky sea salt, such as
  fleur de sel

1 large bag (about 5 ounces)
  unsalted or lightly salted thick-
  sliced potato chips

Preheat the oven to 300 degrees.

Spread the lemon zest on a baking sheet and bake for 5 minutes. Stir the zest and continue to bake until dry to the touch, about 5 minutes more. Remove from the oven and allow the zest to cool completely. Mix with both salts.

Just before serving, preheat the oven to 350 degrees.

Spread the potato chips out on a rimmed baking sheet and bake for 6 to 7 minutes, until glistening. Remove from the oven, sprinkle lightly with lemon salt, and serve warm. The remaining lemon salt can be stored in an airtight container.

Makes ¾ cup lemon salt

FRANK STITT'S ONION DIP

This onion dip was brilliantly reverse-engineered from the standard Lipton dip by chef Frank Stitt of Birmingham, Alabama, who wraps Southern classics in chef techniques and great ingredients. Pretty, it's not. But everyone who tastes it loves it.

Olive oil
1 red onion, thinly sliced
2 cups sour cream
1 tablespoon mascarpone or cream cheese
Scant 1 tablespoon grainy mustard
4 dashes Tabasco, or more to taste

1 tablespoon thinly sliced fresh chives
Juice of ½ lemon
2 dashes Worcestershire sauce
Salt and freshly ground black pepper

Heat a heavy skillet over medium-high heat until hot. Brush the bottom of the pan with olive oil, add the onion, and cook slowly over low heat, stirring often, until deeply browned, almost blackened (do not add any salt). This can take up to 45 minutes. Remove from the heat, and let cool.

Combine the sour cream, mascarpone, mustard, Tabasco, chives, lemon juice, and Worcestershire in a medium bowl. Fold in the onions, then taste and season with salt, pepper, and more Tabasco if necessary. Refrigerate for at least 1 hour, or up to 4 hours, until ready to serve.

Makes 8 to 10 servings

MACARONI AND CHEESE PANCAKES

Kenny Shopsin, one of the few truly scary people I've encountered in the food business, brought forth this Franken-pancake from his famously creative brain. In my first week at my first job in New York, four coworkers invited me to tag along for lunch in the West Village. I trotted along happily in my black silk Eileen Fisher tent dress (oh, the '90s). We didn't know that the owner of Shopsin's was famously hotheaded and—among other brutally enforced rules—never, ever seated more than four people at a table. Soon after Mr. Shopsin started screaming that one of us assholes had to go, I found myself out on the sidewalk alone.

Much later, I read his excellent book, *Eat Me: The Food and Philosophy of Kenny Shopsin*, and understood some of the passion and grief and principle behind the profanity. Still, I'd rather make my own version of these absolutely brilliant pancakes at home.

1½ cups all-purpose flour
1 tablespoon sugar
¼ teaspoon salt
2 teaspoons baking powder
1 teaspoon baking soda
2 large eggs
3 tablespoons butter, melted

1½ cups buttermilk
½ cup grated sharp cheddar
  cheese
About 2 cups leftover macaroni
  and cheese (see page 31)
Maple syrup

Stir together the flour, sugar, salt, baking powder, and baking soda in a large bowl. Whisk the eggs, butter, and buttermilk in another bowl. Add the wet ingredients to the dry and stir gently but thoroughly. Set aside for 10 minutes.

Heat a nonstick griddle or large heavy skillet. Grease the griddle and then for each pancake, place a large pinch of grated cheese on the griddle. Spoon on a pancake's worth of batter and, when it settles, use your fingers to crumble some macaroni and cheese over the top. Adjust the heat so the pancakes cook slowly. Wait until each pancake is covered with bubbles and puffy and dry around the edges, then flip. Cook until browned on the second side. Repeat with the remaining batter. Serve with maple syrup.

Makes about 3 dozen pancakes

SAUSAGE PATTIES

Breakfast for dinner was one of my favorite treats as a kid. And pork sausage and maple syrup is one of those brilliant combinations that always makes you glad to be alive, right up there with asparagus and hollandaise or chocolate and coffee. Serve these with the Macaroni and Cheese Pancakes (page 65) or waffles and coffee ice cream.

1 teaspoon crumbled dried sage
¾ teaspoon salt
¾ teaspoon brown sugar
½ teaspoon freshly ground black
  pepper

½ teaspoon dried thyme
¼ teaspoon red pepper flakes
1 pound coarsely ground pork
  (preferably half belly and half
  butt or shoulder)

Combine the sage, salt, brown sugar, black pepper, thyme, and red pepper flakes in a medium bowl, rubbing them together with your fingers. Add the ground pork and mix lightly but thoroughly. Gently pat the mixture down into the bottom of the bowl, then use a knife to cut it into 6 equal portions. Divide each portion in two and shape them into patties with your hands, making them about ¾ inch thick.

Set an ungreased heavy skillet over low heat, and slowly cook the patties until well browned and cooked through, 15 to 20 minutes. Serve hot.

Makes 12 patties

Note: If grinding the pork yourself, grind the chilled meat in a meat grinder or pulse it in a food processor until finely chopped.

MELON SALAD
WITH CHILES AND MINT

For children, plain ripe melon balls will be quite delicious enough. Set theirs aside before mixing the melon in the dressing. For adults, this spicy-sweet, juicy salad is the perfect counterpoint to rich, eggy brunch food. It's also fantastic with barbecue.

¼ cup fresh lime juice
1 small red chile pepper, such as
   Thai bird or serrano, seeded and
   finely shredded
1 tablespoon superfine sugar

4 cups melon balls from very
   ripe melons, preferably a
   combination of cantaloupe,
   honeydew, and watermelon
10 fresh mint leaves, shredded

Combine the lime juice, chile pepper, and sugar in a large bowl, and stir to dissolve the sugar. Add the melon balls. Refrigerate for at least 1 hour or up to 3 hours, but not overnight (the melon will begin to get mushy).

Just before serving, mix in the mint. Serve cold.

Makes 6 servings

DEVIL DOG CAKE WITH
WHIPPED CREAM FILLING

This tall confection—dark chocolate cake layered with whipped cream and covered with chocolate glaze—is our "house cake" for all birthday events. It steers clear of buttercream frosting, which is highly overrated—usually too greasy and too sweet. And although yellow cake is more birthdayish, it is not a yellow cake, because it is almost impossible to make yellow cake at home with the lightness and softness of a commercial cake or a mix cake.

The perfect yellow cake—spongy, buttery, just barely tangy—has long been a grail object for me, and for some other food-obsessed people I know. My friend Amy finally tasted a worthy one at a bakery in Brooklyn, and she was so excited that she rented out the entire place and hired the baker to teach a class of friends how to make it. Imagine the cries of protest when he said that the recipe provided would not be for his cake, which he would never reveal, but one that would be "easier for home cooks such as yourselves." Needless to say: bakery boycott in effect. If you have the perfect yellow cake recipe, e-mail me at moskin@nytimes.com.

FOR THE CAKE

6 ounces semisweet chocolate, chopped
¾ cup all-purpose flour
¾ cup cake flour
½ teaspoon baking powder
½ teaspoon baking soda
½ teaspoon kosher salt
1¾ cups packed dark brown sugar
6 tablespoons unsalted butter, at room temperature, plus more to grease the pan
1 teaspoon vanilla extract
2 large eggs
¾ cup buttermilk

FOR THE FILLING

2 tablespoons cold water

1 teaspoon unflavored gelatin

1½ cups very cold heavy cream

2 tablespoons confectioners' sugar

½ teaspoon vanilla extract

FOR THE GLAZE

⅔ cup heavy cream

4 ounces bittersweet chocolate, finely chopped

1 tablespoon corn syrup

To make the cake: Preheat the oven to 325 degrees. Butter three 8-inch round cake pans or spray with cooking spray. Line the bottoms with parchment paper rounds and butter or spray the parchment.

Melt the chocolate. Whisk the flours, baking powder, baking soda, and salt in a medium bowl.

In the bowl of a stand mixer, beat the brown sugar, butter, and vanilla together; the mixture will be crumbly. Add the eggs one at a time, beating well after each addition. Beat in the warm melted chocolate. Beat in half of the dry ingredients, then the buttermilk, and then the remaining dry ingredients.

Divide the batter among the prepared pans (if you have one, use a kitchen scale to make sure the batter is evenly distributed).

Bake for 25 to 30 minutes, until a tester inserted into the center of a cake comes out clean. Cool the cakes in the pans for 10 minutes, then turn out onto a rack and peel off the parchment. Let cool completely. (The cake can be made up to 1 day ahead. Wrap the layers in plastic and store at room temperature.)

To make the filling: Put the cold water in a small bowl. Sprinkle the gelatin over it and let stand for 10 minutes to soften.

Bring ½ cup of the cream to a boil in a small heavy saucepan. Add the hot cream to the softened gelatin and stir until it dissolves. Refrigerate, whisking frequently, just until cold, about 5 minutes.

Combine the remaining 1 cup cream, the confectioners' sugar, and vanilla extract in a medium bowl. Using a handheld mixer, beat until soft peaks form. Add the gelatin mixture and beat until firm peaks form.

Place 1 cake layer on a cardboard round or the bottom of a tart pan. Spread half of the filling over it. Top with a second layer and spread the remaining filling over it. Top with the third layer. Chill for at least 3 hours, or overnight.

To make the glaze: Heat the cream to a simmer in a small saucepan over medium heat.

Put the chocolate and corn syrup in a small bowl. Pour the hot cream over the chocolate mixture and stir until smooth.

Pour the glaze onto the center of the chilled cake and let it drip down the sides. Refrigerate for at least 1 hour, or overnight, until ready to serve. Serve on a cake plate.

Makes 1 large layer cake

APRIL

THE FANCY CHALLENGE

THE FANCY CHALLENGE

by **JULIA MOSKIN**

What is a fancy dinner?

"Fancy" is, like "badass" and "crappy," one of many useful words that we *New York Times* reporters are not allowed to use. The copy editors say that it's a meaningless term. I say that everyone knows what "fancy" means: it's something that is openly trying to impress you. Like pornography, fancy is something that we recognize when we see it.

The notion of making sorbet or wearing Louboutin heels "just" to impress someone is so not cool, though we all do it.

But it's OK to try to honor something big—a new baby, or a new boss, or a new year—with a fancy dinner. In food, fancy once meant perfect little canapés and French cheeses; these days, it's homemade sorbet and honey from one's own rooftop hives.

There's been a revolution in "fancy" restaurants in my lifetime, and I'm not even that old. When I was little, china, crystal, and linen were fancy; so were chicken Kiev and quenelles. Now some of New York's most brilliant and desirable restaurants don't have tablecloths, or even chairs. True hospitality, the art of making people feel not only comfortable but well taken care of, has become the point.

So the key moment of the fancy dinner isn't when the foie gras is served—

it's when the guests arrive. As long as the host isn't having a nervous breakdown around the dinner, this realization will make everyone happy.

So what to cook? Here are a few hard-won lessons:

- ✗ A stew is not fancy, no matter how delicious it might be.
- ✗ Pasta is not fancy, simply because it is ubiquitous (and don't bother with the angry letters, I am familiar with the vastness of the Italian pasta repertoire).
- ✗ Roast chicken with truffles stuffed under the skin is not fancy—because, really, truffles with roast chicken is just a waste of both.

On the other hand:

- ✗ Roast chicken can be fancy if it is stuffed with something delicious.
- ✗ Soup can be fancy if it isn't chunky.
- ✗ Salad can be fancy if it lies down on a plate and behaves.

One of the great things about New York City is that people are absolutely bowled over when a home cook shows even minimal effort. At restaurants, our standards are different. Restaurants are paid to carve my beets into the shape of a lotus flower, tweeze my salad into fluffy perfection, fold my napkin. Thus, I am merciless in my expectations. But when a hospitable friend simply marinates a leg of lamb for me, I am practically moved to tears.

Severson is one of the most fancy-fearing people I know. It's not that she doesn't understand the value of making an effort; she gets hung up on the small stuff. Before a dinner party, she turns into Betty Draper in chinos, sweating over each sprig of cilantro. I attribute this anxiety to her time living in the Bay Area, where competitive home cooking seems to be a second career. If you see her, tell he to relax. She hates that.

PECAN CHEESE CRISPS

The quest for the perfect cheese crisp has occupied me for many years. Once I had mastered the perfect cheese puff (see Gougères, page 17), I still felt a need for a melting but crisp little cracker that would give the savory effect of a Cheese Nip in a much nicer package. Do not reduce the amount of cayenne—it adds only a gentle kick and brings out the cheese flavor in a big way. But feel free to increase it.

8 tablespoons (1 stick) unsalted
   butter, at room temperature

8 ounces orange cheddar cheese,
   coarsely grated (2 cups)

1 large egg yolk

½ teaspoon salt

½ teaspoon cayenne pepper

⅔ cup all-purpose flour

⅔ cup pecans, finely chopped

Position a rack in the middle of the oven and preheat the oven to 350 degrees. Butter two baking sheets.

In the bowl of a stand mixer, use the paddle attachment and beat together the butter and cheese until very smooth. Beat in the remaining ingredients.

Roll rounded teaspoons of the dough into balls and arrange 3 inches apart on the buttered baking sheets. (Or, form the dough into 2 logs, 1½ inches in diameter. Freeze until firm, or for up to 3 months. Slice ¼ inch thick.)

Bake in batches until golden, 15 to 18 minutes. Let cool on a rack.

Makes 3 to 4 dozen crisps

FENNEL SALAD WITH
GREEN APPLES AND LEMON ZEST

The key to fennel salad is in the slicing. Knife skills, along with a list of all the valid two-letter words in Scrabble and a starter apartment, are among the most valuable gifts my parents have given me.

Fennel makes a delicious, tender salad when very thinly sliced, not difficult to do with a sharp knife. Although it is heretical to say this in the food world, a person might buy cheap knives, wash them in the dishwasher, and replace them when they get dull. This person might feel a little guilty, but it is better than not cooking at all.

2 medium fennel bulbs
2 tart firm apples, such as pippins
  or Granny Smith, or pears, such
  as Bosc
½ cup finely shaved Pecorino
  Romano or Manchego cheese
Grated zest of 1 lemon

¼ cup extra-virgin olive oil, plus
  more for drizzling
2 tablespoons chopped fresh
  parsley
Salt and freshly ground black
  pepper

Cut the stalks off the fennel. Coarsely chop a handful of the dark green fronds and reserve. Discard the stalks and remaining fronds. Cut each fennel bulb in half, top to bottom, then cut crosswise into very thin slices. Soak in a bowl of cold water in the refrigerator until ready to use, or up to 8 hours.

Core the apples but do not peel them. Slice them very thin and toss with the drained fennel slices in a bowl. Add the cheese, zest, olive oil, and parsley. Toss again, then season to taste with salt and pepper.

Transfer to a serving bowl, sprinkle with the reserved fennel, and drizzle with more olive oil. Serve on chilled salad plates.

Makes 6 to 8 servings

LAMB RACK WITH
CILANTRO-MINT CRUST

My "Eat Club" is a group of women who have been chowhounding around New York's outer boroughs since before the Internet. (We had to do our research in magazines and newspapers—imagine.) Of dozens of expeditions over almost two decades, one of the most memorable for me was our discovery of the deliciousness of lamb fat. In a Central Asian kebab house in Queens, I ate an entire kebab of clean-tasting, gorgeously browned fat from the tail of a sheep.

It was then that I realized that I had been cooking lamb all wrong, trimming off every bit of the fat before cooking, in a misguided manner. Leaving the fat on the chops makes this a succulent, bone-sucking entrée. But the high quality of domestic lamb and the breathtaking price of the racks keep it fancy.

3 racks of lamb, not Frenched, with ½-inch layer of fat left on	3 tablespoons finely chopped fresh mint
Salt and freshly ground black pepper	3 tablespoons finely chopped fresh cilantro
3 tablespoons olive oil	¾ teaspoon finely chopped garlic
¾ cup fresh bread crumbs	1 tablepoon finely chopped shallot

Let the lamb come to room temperature.

Preheat the oven to 500 degrees and the broiler to high. Meanwhile, season the lamb with salt and pepper and arrange meat side down on a rimmed baking sheet. Brush with 1½ tablespoons of the olive oil. Set aside.

Toss together the bread crumbs, herbs, garlic, shallot, and the remaining 1½ tablespoons olive oil in a bowl.

Broil the racks until the fat is browned and sizzling, about 3 minutes. Turn the racks over and repeat.

Pull the lamb out of the broiler (or turn the broiler off) and sprinkle the bread crumb mixture over the top. Bake at 500 degrees for 8 to 10 minutes, until well browned on the outside and pink (not red) in the center. Let rest for at least 5 minutes before slicing into chops and serving.

Makes 6 servings

ROASTED BRUSSELS SPROUTS
WITH PAPRIKA AND PISTACHIOS

As far as I'm concerned, the invention of the roasted Brussels sprout is up there with over-the-counter Ibuprofen and wedge boots: a small step for civilization that has truly made my life better. The secret is that you have to cut them in half, so the liquid inside evaporates in the oven. Brussels sprouts, roasted whole, have all the appeal of hot wet golf balls.

Unlike potatoes and carrots, it is possible to overdo roasting with Brussels sprouts, as they can become bitter and leathery. Sometimes 15 minutes in the oven is all it takes to turn the edges crisp and fragrant. If serving with the lamb, roast the sprouts just before cooking the meat.

2 pounds Brussels sprouts,
   trimmed and halved lengthwise,
   or quartered if large
3 tablespoons vegetable oil
1 teaspoon sweet paprika—
   smoked if desired

1 teaspoon salt
2 tablespoons unsalted butter,
   melted
2 tablespoons coarsely chopped
   pistachios (optional)

Position a rack in the upper third of the oven and preheat the oven to 425 degrees (if the oven has a convection setting, use it).

Toss the sprouts, oil, paprika, and salt together, then arrange the sprouts cut side down on a large rimmed baking sheet. (Or just toss everything together on the baking sheet.) Roast, without turning, for 20 minutes, or until the outer leaves are tender and just turning brown. Drizzle with the butter, sprinkle with the nuts, if using, and toss to coat. Continue roasting for 5 to 15 minutes, until the sprouts are dark brown. Serve hot or warm.

Makes 6 to 8 servings

CHOCOLATE LOG

Long, long ago, before the molten chocolate cake took over the earth, American cooks were whipping egg whites for the soft flourless cake layer of this timeless dessert. They did so because of Dione Lucas, an elegant, Cordon-Bleu-trained Englishwoman who was America's first TV cook, long before Julia Child and The Galloping Gourmet (whom I always feared as a child, just from his name).

This chocolate log was one of her signature dishes, but I use Jacques Pépin's cake recipe because it rolls more easily. Christmas-type people often serve this as a bûche de Noël, but I make it any time of year. (In our house, we just call it "The Log.") And I have adjusted for modern tastes: better chocolate, more vanilla.

FOR THE CAKE

1 cup heavy cream

8 ounces bittersweet chocolate, finely chopped

7 large egg whites, at room temperature

3 tablespoons sugar

¼ teaspoon salt

FOR THE FILLING

1 cup very cold heavy cream

1½ tablespoons sugar

1 teaspoon vanilla extract

Unsweetened Dutch-process cocoa powder

Confectioners' sugar

To make the cake: Position a rack in the center of the oven and preheat the oven to 350 degrees. Butter a large rimmed baking sheet (about 13 inches by 18 inches) and line with parchment or waxed paper, letting the paper hang over the ends by 2 inches.

Heat the cream to a simmer in a medium saucepan. Add the chocolate and stir vigorously with a small whisk to melt the chocolate quickly. Immediately remove from the heat.

Whip the egg whites, sugar, and salt in a mixer just until stiff and glossy. Scoop a spoonful of the egg whites into the chocolate mixture and stir to blend. Then pour the chocolate mixture into the egg whites and fold together with a rubber spatula until smooth (there may still be some streak of white visible).

Pour the batter into the pan and spread it evenly. Bake for 10 to 14 minutes, until set and puffed. Using the ends of the paper, lift out the cake, transfer to a rack, and let cool to room temperature.

To fill and roll the cake: Whip the cream with the sugar and vanilla until it just holds stiff peaks. Spread evenly over the cake.

Put a platter next to a long side of the cake. Using the paper as an aid, beginning with a long side, roll up the cake jelly roll-style. Carefully transfer the roll, seam side down, to the platter, using the paper to help it slide. (It might crack but it will still hold together.)

Dust the cake generously with cocoa powder and confectioners' sugar. Refrigerate at least 1 hour or overnight. Slice and serve.

Makes 8 to 10 servings

APRIL

THE FANCY CHALLENGE

by **KIM SEVERSON**

Seeing us side by side, you might look at Ms. Moskin and think, "She's the fancy one." You would be right. So when it came to our battle over dinner for six, I got a little edgy. Even the phrase "dinner party" sounded too fancy for me.

Don't get me wrong. I assure you it pays to have the chops to put on a special, intimate, and seemingly luxurious dinner party. More than just having a few friends over, a formal dinner party is an event. It marks something beyond simple camaraderie. A dinner party is a way to introduce your new girlfriend to your friends, to get closer to your pending in-laws, to celebrate promotions, to feel like a grown-up. It is a way to add a heightened sense of importance to the daily ritual of communion over a meal.

Also, it's fun. People inclined to hamminess (I'm talking to myself here) love a tableful of people to make laugh. People who are shy in social situations can find refuge in the orchestrated rhythms of a dinner party or slip into the kitchen to help you. And, best of all, you don't have to deal with the horrors of the potluck or logistical challenges of a cocktail party (for party tips, see The Open-House Challenge, page 259).

My worry, in facing down Moskin, was that my life is just not fancy enough. I

serve my food on old Fiestaware. Moskin has flatware with a pedigree. I find little joy in the language of the French culinary canon, which Moskin speaks with ease. I am not a sous-vide girl, nor one to make the puff pastry in which to coddle a beef Wellington.

The challenge, then, was to find a way to make people feel cared for and special but stay in my own skin. I can't keep up with Miss Fancy Pants, and I'm not going to go through the culinary gymnastics people might expect from someone who writes about food.

The solution is to make time my luxury ingredient.

When it comes to food, time is the new luxury. Food that might be simple to execute but takes a long time to produce has acquired a new value on our tables. Having time to wander a farmers' market can feel like an indulgence. Salami is the new black truffle—simple food that's special not because it is expensive, but because it requires time and attention. To test my theory, make a batch of jam and give it to your friends. It beats a jar of expensive salt or an imported cheese every time.

I have also planned a meal that requires little last-minute work and allows me to offer guests my own time. It's based on dishes that have been made delicious with time, like thin, buttery slices of potato seasoned with whole bay leaves that take an hour to crisp and pork that is simmered for hours in milk, lemon, and sage.

I love that old hostess trick where you get everything done with fifteen minutes to spare, using the last bit of time to sit down and have a drink and take a breath. It's so much better to greet guests looking all chill. (What, me stressed? Ha ha ha!)

Just before my guests arrive I warm a small sauté pan filled with a mix of olives, a strip of orange peel, a few sprigs of thyme, a garlic clove, and a dried chile. The olives will be ready to set on the table, along with an excellent chicken liver pâté, to get things started.

I like to serve all my food on platters at the center of the table. I know people will argue that the food can cool by the time everyone gets served, but taking the time to pass platters and making sure your neighbor's plate is full creates a sense of community that is worth losing a few degrees of heat.

And I always offer a few words of gratitude before we all eat.

With the coffee ready to start brewing, the apple tart set to serve, and a few of my favorite store-bought caramels or chocolates on a blue Fiestaware plate, it all feels pretty damn luxurious.

CHICKEN LIVER PÂTÉ

This is a delicious spread, silky with butter, that came from Jacques Pépin. I have made it without the Cognac, and it is still good. To be perfect, though, it requires you to search out good livers from well-raised chickens. You're giving your guests the gift of time, remember? I like it on very crispy toasts, which are best made with lightly buttered thin slices of baguette baked on a baking sheet at 325 degrees for 6 minutes or until they are golden brown but not so crisp that they will shatter.

8 ounces chicken livers, well trimmed
½ small onion, thinly sliced
1 small garlic clove, smashed and peeled
1 bay leaf
¼ teaspoon fresh thyme leaves
Kosher salt

½ cup water
12 tablespoons (1½ sticks) unsalted butter, at room temperature
2 teaspoons Cognac or other brandy
Freshly ground black pepper

Combine the chicken livers, onion, garlic, bay leaf, thyme, and ½ teaspoon salt in a medium saucepan, add the water, and bring to a simmer. Cover, reduce the heat to low, and cook, stirring occasionally, until the livers are just barely pink inside, about 3 minutes. Remove from the heat and let stand, covered, for 5 minutes.

Discard the bay leaf. Using a slotted spoon, transfer the livers, onion, and garlic to a food processor; process until coarsely pureed. With the machine on, add the butter 2 tablespoons at a time, processing until incorporated. Add the Cognac, season with salt and pepper, and process until completely smooth.

Scrape the pâté into two or three ramekins. Press a piece of plastic wrap directly against the surface of the pâté and refrigerate until firm. (If you want to make this a few days ahead, pour a thin layer of melted butter over the top and wrap in plastic.)

Makes 6 servings

THE BEST KALE SALAD

Kale, which got big in 2011, is one of the most versatile greens in my rotation. It's easy to grow and easy to sauté with a little vinegar or to roast into chips (see page 132). Lacinato kale, also called Tuscan or black kale, is what you want for this salad. Look for bunches that are so fresh and plump they almost seem juicy. Limp kale won't do. And though you can use regular lemons, Meyer lemons give the dressing more depth.

1 large bunch lacinato (Tuscan) kale

1 large shallot, finely chopped

Juice of 1 large Meyer lemon (about 3 tablespoons)

Salt

⅓ cup olive oil, or more

1 cup coarsely shredded ricotta salata

Freshly ground black pepper

Trim the thick stems from the bottom of the kale leaves. Stack the leaves (a few at a time), roll them up like a cigar, and thinly slice crosswise to make lovely ribbons.

Mix together the shallot, lemon juice, and about ¼ teaspoon salt in a small bowl. Whisk in the olive oil and taste; the dressing should be fairly tart. Add a bit more olive oil or lemon juice to adjust the flavor.

Toss the kale with the dressing in a large bowl. Add the cheese and taste again, adding a little pepper and more salt if it needs it.

Makes 6 servings

PORK BRAISED
IN MILK AND CREAM

On the surface, this dish might sound horrible, but if you are confident enough and patient enough, the reward is a sauce that is so good it nearly made Moskin's husband leave her for me. (She, for the record, recoiled in horror at the idea of the recipe. She had an unfortunate pork-and-milk experience as a young cook.)

The recipe is a classic Italian one. It leans on the magic of heat and lemon to produce delicious golden curds, which you then strain into a rich, magical sauce.

Various chefs have put forth versions of the recipe—this one is an amalgam, tweaked after some experimentation.

One 2½- to 3-pound pork loin roast
Kosher salt and freshly ground
  black pepper
1 tablespoon chopped garlic, plus
  5 large garlic cloves, slightly
  crushed and peeled
1 tablespoon chopped fresh sage,
  plus leaves from 2 or 3 fresh sage
  sprigs

2 tablespoons olive oil
3 cups milk
3 cups heavy cream
2 lemons
3 tablespoons unsalted butter

ALICE'S APPLE TART
WITH WHIPPED CREAM

This comes from the team at Chez Panisse, which has written great books about fruit and desserts. I eat at Alice's restaurant as often as I can, and especially love being in the kitchen, where the Zen of cooking makes me realize I am probably never going to get it right. Still, one tries. Go free-form on this tart, using a large baking sheet rather than a tart pan. Don't worry that the apple slices aren't perfectly arranged, unless that's your thing. To save time, whip your cream before your guests arrive, then add in a good spoon or two of crème fraîche or plain yogurt at the end. That way, it can sit in the refrigerator until dessert time without getting all weepy.

1 cup unbleached all-purpose
   flour
½ teaspoon granulated sugar
⅛ teaspoon salt
6 tablespoons unsalted butter,
   cut into ½-inch pieces and
   chilled
3½ tablespoons cold water
2 pounds firm apples (Granny
   Smith or Pink Ladies), peeled,
   cored, and thinly sliced; cores
   and peels reserved
2 tablespoons unsalted butter,
   melted

¼ cup sugar (preferably coarse,
   but granulated will do)

FOR THE GLAZE
The reserved apple cores and peels

½ cup sugar

FOR THE CREAM
1 pint heavy cream
½ teaspoon vanilla extract

1 heaping tablespoon crème
   fraîche or plain yogurt

To make the tart: Combine the flour, granulated sugar, and salt in a food processor or the bowl of a stand mixer. (This can be done by hand too, but it's not as easy.) Add about half the chilled butter and pulse or mix to turn the whole thing into something that is the texture of coarse sand. Add the rest of the chilled butter and mix just so you're left with some large pieces of butter. Dribble in a teaspoon or so of water, stir, and then add a bit more water. Keep mixing with your hands, adding a bit more water until the whole thing suddenly holds together in a scraggly ball. Flatten into a 4-inch disk and refrigerate for 30 minutes or longer.

When ready to roll out the dough, pull it out and let it sit for 10 minutes or so. You want it cold but soft enough to roll.

Position a rack in the center of the oven and preheat the oven to 400 degrees. Line a large baking sheet with parchment.

Lightly flour a counter and roll out the dough into a large circle about 14 inches across. Place the dough on the baking sheet (the edges will extend over the sides of the pan; that's OK). Arrange the apples on the dough in circles, leaving a border of 2 or 3 inches. Fold the edges of the dough over the apples.

Brush the entire top of the tart with the melted butter. Sprinkle 1 tablespoon of the coarse sugar over the dough rim, then sprinkle the remaining coarse sugar over the apples. Bake for about 45 minutes, or until deep golden brown, turning the pan every 15 minutes, until the apples are soft with browned edges and the crust has caramelized.

To make the glaze: Meanwhile, combine the peels, cores, and sugar in a saucepan, add just enough water to cover, and bring to a simmer. Simmer for 25 minutes. Strain the glaze.

Let the tart cool for 15 minutes, then brush with the glaze.

To make the whipped cream: In a chilled bowl, add the cream and vanilla and use a hand mixer to bring the mixture to a soft peak stage. Stir in the crème fraîche or yogurt. You can do this a couple of hours ahead. Stir to refresh just before serving.

Serve the tart with the chilled whipped cream.

Makes 1 large tart

MAY

THE MOTHERS' CHALLENGE

JULIA'S MENU

Smoked Salmon and Cucumbers
with Raspberry Vinaigrette
Rosemary-Cornflake Chicken
Not My Grandmother's Brisket
Baby Carrots with Black Olives
Labor-Saving Orange Cake

MAY

THE MOTHERS' CHALLENGE

by **KIM SEVERSON**

My mother, Anne Marie Zappa Severson, loved the convenience of the supermarket. And why not? The daughter of Italian immigrants and one of the youngest of eleven siblings, she grew up on a dairy farm. The family didn't have a refrigerator until she was well into elementary school.

They ate all parts of the pig, and that included letting pans of blood congeal into pudding. My mother spent a childhood making countless trips to the root cellar and drinking heroic amounts of raw milk.

But then came nirvana: the modern American supermarket.

Once out of the house and married, she filled her cart with already-butchered chickens on white foam trays, cans of soup, and bags of frozen vegetables—and even (and I gulp here) jars of "Italian seasoning." These were the prizes that came with a suburban housewife's life.

This is not to say she couldn't cook. The woman was a machine. Every day, she had to feed five kids and a husband three squares. But her real education came in the competitive world of the volunteer life. The Welcome Wagon, the hospital auxiliary, the Junior League. Countless dishes to take to the neighbors. She was a prolific contributor to the various community cookbooks produced in the cities we lived in, as my dad's job took us around the country. All of that was the training ground for my mother's cooking skills.

We kids, of course, were the beneficiaries. One was well advised not to miss dinner, which on any given night might center on some impossibly fancy recipe from a women's magazine or a simple meat loaf. On Christmas, she set a big prime rib on the elegant dining room table for my dad to carve.

As the eldest daughter, I was singled out for private cooking lessons. I could dress a salad before I'd mastered fractions. I helped make the spaghetti sauce and got to whip the cream. I learned the magic of cream puffs and the delight of fried chicken livers (Mom was from peasant farm stock, after all).

The best thing I learned, though, was how to run an economical kitchen. Mom had to make do. For a time, we drank powdered milk mixed with water and just a little of the real thing. The bits and pieces in the vegetable bin became minestrone soup. We ate radishes from my dad's garden and venison from his hunting trips.

And at least once a week, Mom filled out our plates with something my brothers still call greasy spaghetti. You might see this on a menu as spaghetti *aglio olio*. A simple, immensely satisfying dish of pasta, olive oil, and garlic.

But I never felt like I wanted for anything.

Of course, this was a life far away from Ms. Moskin's Upper West Side existence, with its fancy French knives and *Silver Palate* Chicken Marbella.

After all, how can one compete with a girl named after Julia Child?

Very well, I think.

PRIME RIB WITH POPOVERS

For more than forty years, the smell of smoking beef fat filled our house every Christmas. After Mass, my mom would prepare a prime rib of beef using this particular method. It never seemed as if it would work, but it does, like magic, no matter how large or small your roast. Mom always said the key was the quality of the roast, and that was something you could never tell until you put a bite in your mouth. It was fate, as if some kind of divine power decided whether the prime rib was going to be any good that year. There is something to that, especially when one dabbles with pasture-raised beef.

For this recipe, I prefer meat from a humanely raised and butchered animal, but I try to get one that has at least been finished on grain. The quality of the beef fat is better and certainly more consistent, and that makes for better popovers.

Several fat garlic cloves or more	Olive oil
Salt	Freshly ground black pepper
A beef prime rib—1 bone per person	Popovers (recipe follows)

Depending on the size of the roast, you will need at least 3 big garlic cloves, probably more. A clove a pound is not a bad guide. Make a paste with the garlic and salt by chopping the garlic, then adding a teaspoon or so of salt for each fat clove and working them both into a paste with the side of the knife against the cutting board.

Place the roast in a large roasting pan bone side down, so the bones act as a rack. Make some small cuts all over the fat cap, then rub the roast with olive oil. Follow by massaging the garlic mixture into the meat and fat. Let the roast sit for about an hour before roasting. Season with pepper.

Preheat the oven to 500 degrees.

Put the roast in the oven and set the timer, allowing 6½ minutes per pound for a roast that is rare in the middle, with some medium-rare meat and a bit of medium meat at the ends (a 4-pound roast, for example, would cook for 26 minutes).

Turn off the oven and warn everyone in the house not to open the oven door under any circumstance, on the penalty of death.

After 2 hours, remove the roast. Set it on a platter and reserve the fat for the popovers.

Let the roast rest while you make the popovers, then carve and serve with the popovers.

Popovers

The key to this recipe is beef fat. You might not have enough from the roast, but that, while sad, is not a deal breaker. Just use melted butter to make up the difference. Also, it's essential to make sure the muffin cups are well greased and that the oven has been properly preheated. And serve them right away.

1½ cups milk	1½ teaspoons kosher salt
1½ cups all-purpose flour	¼ cup rendered beef fat or melted
4 large eggs	butter, or a combination

Position a rack in the lower third of the oven and preheat the oven to 425 degrees. Heat a 12-cup muffin tin in the oven.

Meanwhile, mix together everything except 1½ tablespoons of the beef fat. You can do this with a hand mixer, a blender, or a whisk and a strong arm. The batter should be very smooth.

Remove the hot muffin pan and add about ½ teaspoon of the remaining beef fat to each cup. Put the pan back in the oven for about 5 minutes. The fat needs to be very hot.

Working quickly, divide the batter among the muffin cups and put the pan in the oven. Bake for 20 minutes. Be patient—don't peek. Then drop the heat to 350 degrees and continue to bake for about 18 minutes more. The popovers should be puffy and deeply golden. Serve immediately.

Makes 12 servings

ITALIAN GREEN SALAD
WITH VINAIGRETTE

One of my first kitchen tasks was cleaning lettuce. I would stack the leaves and tear them into pieces, trying to get as many done at once so I could go back and play. "You're tearing those like a phone book!" my mother would scold. The key, she taught me, was to be gentle and patient, treating each leaf with some respect. Later Alice Waters tried to teach me the same thing.

A good salad begins and ends with perfect lettuce. Fill a sink with cold water and add the leaves. Any mix will do, but young spring lettuces are a favorite. The point is to have a nice variety, so the salad will be interesting to eat. My mother, of course, used mostly iceberg and sometimes, to be fancy, radicchio. I still like the crunch of iceberg or romaine in a green salad, supported by the color and flavor of garden lettuces.

The dressing should be simple, slightly acidic, and subtle. My mother simply added oil, tossed in salt and pepper, and then finished with good old-fashioned supermarket red wine vinegar, never measuring but always hitting the proportions just right.

This dressing recipe is based on what Alice Waters uses, though she prefers garlic to shallots. It will dress enough salad for four people, but the quantity can vary. The key is to dress lightly, taste a leaf, and add more. It's a recipe that you can easily make more or less of depending on the size of your guest list.

1 medium shallot
Kosher salt
2 tablespoons red wine vinegar
¼ cup olive oil
Freshly ground black pepper
A mix of good lettuces (allow
 about 2 heaping cups per
 person) gently washed and dried

Chop the shallot as fine as possible and then, using the side of the knife, press in 2 big pinches of salt. Scrape into a small bowl and whisk in the vinegar. Slowly whisk in the olive oil. Grind in some pepper, whisk again, and taste for seasoning.

Toss with the greens just before serving.

Makes 4 servings

Arugula
Hot, peppery tastes, best at 2.5".
Plant grows to 12-18" before bolting.
Leaves small, light yellow flowers.
Plus vitamins, minerals
Source of calcium, potassium,
Vitamin C and A.
Prefers cool weather.

6 pk
4.50

MINESTRONE

This is the go-to soup my mother made for spaghetti dinners, or when she was trying to fancy up other meals. My sister-in-law, Carleen Jeffry, has been working on the recipe in her California kitchen. "Of course, it's never as good as when she is here to supervise. I have sometimes called it 'kitchen sink' soup, because I throw in whatever I need to use up from my refrigerator. So you can always substitute what you have on hand for these veggies." Good advice.

4 ounces salt pork or bacon, finely chopped
¼ cup olive oil, plus more for drizzling
1 large white or yellow onion, chopped
2 celery stalks, chopped
2 carrots, chopped
3 garlic cloves, chopped
½ teaspoon dried oregano
½ teaspoon dried basil
¼ teaspoon dried thyme
2 zucchini, chopped
Salt and freshly ground black pepper
One 14-ounce can diced Italian tomatoes
4 cups chicken or vegetable stock, homemade is best but canned will work
One 14-ounce can cannellini beans, drained and rinsed
About 2 ounces spaghetti, broken into 1-inch-long pieces

½ cup chopped fresh flat-leaf parsley leaves, plus more for garnish
Chopped fresh basil (optional)

Sauté the salt pork in the olive oil in a large soup pot just until it's cooked and has rendered some fat but is not crisp. Add the onion and sauté for 2 to 3 minutes. Add the celery, carrots, and garlic. Rub the oregano, basil, and thyme between the palms of your hands to release their flavor and add to the pot. Sauté for 2 to 3 minutes, then add the zucchini, stir to combine, and add salt and pepper to taste. Sauté for 2 to 3 minutes more. If the mixture seems dry, add a bit more olive oil.

Add the tomatoes and broth, bring to a simmer, and let simmer for about 15 minutes. Add the beans, spaghetti, and parsley, adjust the salt and pepper, and cook until the spaghetti is al dente, about 11 minutes.

Ladle the soup into bowls and top each with a swirl of olive oil and a sprinkling of chopped parsley or of basil, if, as my mother would say, "You've got a little lying around."

Makes 4 main-course or 6 appetizer servings

GREASY SPAGHETTI

This is a perfect side dish when you are cooking a simple steak. It's also perfect if you are poor, in college, or simply up late and in need of a bowl of pasta. You can easily omit the bread crumbs, which is what my mother often did when she was in a hurry to feed our family of seven.

4 tablespoons butter
½ cup fresh bread crumbs
1 pound spaghetti
½ cup extra-virgin olive oil
4 garlic cloves, finely chopped

1 teaspoon red pepper flakes, or to taste
Salt and freshly ground black pepper
Freshly grated Parmesan cheese

Melt the butter in a saucepan. Add the bread crumbs and toast until the bread is golden brown. Set aside.

Cook the spaghetti in a large pot of boiling well-salted water for about 8 minutes; be careful to not overcook it. Drain, reserving about a cup of the water.

Meanwhile, heat the olive oil in a sauté pan large enough to hold the spaghetti. Toss in the garlic and sauté over medium heat until it just starts to turn golden, about 4 minutes. Add the red pepper flakes.

Add the spaghetti to the sauce and turn several times to combine. Add ¼ cup or more of the pasta water, so the mixture is moist but not soupy. Season with salt and pepper.

Toss with the toasted bread crumb mixture and serve. Pass Parmesan cheese at the table.

Makes 4 to 6 servings

CHOCOLATE POTS DE CRÈME

My mother was the master of the community cookbook. We moved so much, she had to find ways to get in with the neighbors quickly. Put together in the days when women stayed at home more and did plenty of volunteer work, these cookbooks mark a time in history I often long for. My mother was on the cookbook committee for *More Steamboat Simmers* (1986), recipes from the home cooks of Steamboat Springs, Colorado, where my parents now live. My copy lives alongside the dozens of other community cookbooks I have collected over the years and this recipe is from that. It's easy, and my mother served it for years, even when her Parkinson's made it hard to cook but she was having the bridge group over. It's an indelible memory for me.

¾ cup milk

One 6-ounce package chocolate chips

2 tablespoons sugar

1 large egg

Pinch of salt

1 tablespoon rum or vanilla extract

Whipped cream (optional)

Chocolate curls (optional)

Heat the milk to just under a boil.

Put all the remaining ingredients in a blender. Add the milk and blend on low for 1 minute.

Pour into six small glasses or cups and chill for at least 2 hours. This can be made 2 days ahead.

Top with whipped cream and chocolate curls, optional.

Makes 6 servings

THE MOTHERS' CHALLENGE

by JULIA MOSKIN

Very often, the first (and only) thing I say when asked, "How did you become a food writer?" is this:

"My parents named me after Julia Child."

Really, what more is there to say? In the 1960s, when I was born, both my parents were infatuated with cooking. As "young marrieds" (a common phrase in that far-off time), they cooked their way through *Mastering the Art of French Cooking.*

If Severson is a formidable adversary in the kitchen, I live in fear of her mother. A woman who raises five children without resorting to takeout on a near-daily basis is more impressive to me than any top-toque chef, and that is the truth. What does the chef have as a support system? A sous-chef or twelve, an assistant, and probably a wife to hold down the fort at home. The mother, on a good day, has a working dishwasher and a kid old enough to cut cherry tomatoes in half.

But my mom had a secret weapon: my dad.

Cooking was not "women's work" at our house, for which I am grateful. So many cooks cite their mothers as teachers; I feel lucky that my parents started out together in the kitchen, stayed there because they enjoyed it, and taught my sister and me by example. Guided by Elizabeth David, Richard Olney, and the *Time-Life* series, they cooked together. And, more important for my later career, ate out constantly.

By the summer of love, 1968, my parents had been married for three years and I was a year old. Their apartment kitchen, still unchanged as I write, housed a massive black restaurant stove with six burners, two ovens, a broiler, and a griddle, relics of one of my grandfather's many defunct businesses. While their friends learned to smoke pot and got divorced and marched on Washington and raised their consciousnesses, they mainly did two things: they stayed home, and they cooked dinner.

In the 1970s, broken glass still crunched underfoot on the Upper West Side, and the people who lived there seemed to fit easily into just a few categories: college students; recent immigrants from Puerto Rico, Taiwan, and Ireland; classical musicians; and thousands of Jews, from the tattooed Holocaust survivor who waxed women's legs at my mother's salon to the Zabar family, who were and are local royalty. And it was a very Jewish universe, except for the occasional Cuban-Chinese restaurant or pizza joint, a fact that I took for granted at the time: I thought that's what all cities were like.

All the way across town, my grandmother Fannie and her mother, Ida, who had arrived in the United States together in 1921 from a shtetl in the Ukraine lived in a deluxe apartment in a high-rise with a swimming pool on the roof. As you might expect of someone who grew up with dirt floors and no running water, Fannie was determined to avoid domestic drudgery. She abandoned the kitchen as soon as she earned enough to pay a cook (though Ida still sneaked into the kitchen to make jellied calves' feet and gefilte fish). For her daughter, Hanna, going back into the kitchen was a form of rebellion.

My parents made beef Wellington in their first studio apartment, washing all the pots and bowls in the bathtub. And my father still remembers the shame of not having enough money to cover the cost of the first veal scaloppini he ever tried to buy, at the fancy butcher on Madison Avenue.

They still use the carbon-steel knives that they bought in 1968—one of the indicators, I have come to realize, that my parents are children not only of the 1950s, when they came of age, but also of the 1930s, when their own parents did. When my father was young, his family was prosperous enough to eat dinner at

restaurants or the golf club occasionally—but to save money, they would have an appetizer of tomato juice or Jell-O at home beforehand. Depression-era frugality also lives on in my mother's habit of keeping salami ends, stale bread, and even the most minute quantities of leftover food. It must be admitted, however, that extraordinary meals have been assembled from some of those scraps.

Ultimately, they both became excellent eaters and cooks in ways that reflect their personalities. They'll eat anywhere, try anything, and together, their taste in food is infallible.

My father is cautious, a recipe follower and methodical to the point of madness, a master of the mise-en-place. He has developed an internal GPS that positions every meal he eats, from kebabs in Turkey to Yucatecan tacos, in comparison to the serviceable bistro three blocks from their apartment. "Was it better than French Roast?" is all I need to ask.

My mother has only to enter a kitchen for it to explode, with vegetables all over the place, spice drawers open, refrigerator contents spilled out on the floor. Long after the appointed dinner hour, the kitchen boils over and spits out a glorious meal, my mother running behind each platter with a saltcellar, a fistful of parsley, and another of lemon wedges. That, to me, is cooking.

SMOKED SALMON AND CUCUMBERS
WITH RASPBERRY VINAIGRETTE

I have lots of culinary mothers who made me the cook (and writer) I am today, even though I know them only through their books: the earthy Paula Wolfert; the rigorous and nostalgic Mimi Sheraton; the earnest Deborah Madison; the fragrant Yamuna Devi; and the playful Laurie Colwin. This dish is the creation of Barbara Kafka, a food writer who I think of as my culinary grandmother, despite the fact that we've never met.

I've always been a fiend for vinegar, going back to the pasta salad I invented in middle school when cold fusilli was all the rage. It included broccoli florets and leftover roast chicken from Zabar's, as well as the pasta, all dressed with straight balsamic. My sister and I would eat it with tears streaming down our cheeks, gasping for air but somehow in love. This vinaigrette was also trendy in the 1980s, when raspberry vinegar and pink peppercorns had just arrived on the scene, but it has stood the test of time. My mother makes it constantly, and it is always greeted with ecstasy. In small portions, smoked salmon is not as filling as you might think and thus makes a good first course.

1½ tablespoons raspberry vinegar
1 tablespoon fresh lemon juice
1 tablespoon crushed pink
  peppercorns
1 tablespoon thinly sliced fresh
  chives, plus extra for garnish
Salt and freshly ground black
  pepper

3 tablespoons olive oil
6 ounces thinly sliced smoked
  salmon
1 large or 2 small cucumbers,
  thinly sliced

Whisk the vinegar, lemon juice, peppercorns, and chives together in a small bowl. Sprinkle with salt and pepper. Whisk in the oil; taste and adjust the seasonings. Set aside.

Arrange the salmon and cucumber slices attractively on salad plates. (I usually lay the salmon across the center and put the cucumbers on each side.) Use a spoon to dribble the vinaigrette over the salads. Sprinkle with chives and black pepper and serve immediately, or within 30 minutes.

Makes 4 to 6 servings

ROSEMARY-CORNFLAKE CHICKEN

This community-cookbook recipe comes from my elementary school, where my mother worked as the librarian. The New York City public school system of the 1970s is now regarded with horror, but at the time, we didn't know how underserved we were. Until middle school, when things did get pretty feral, everyone got along fine: the kids from the projects, the flower children, and the sprouts of local intellectuals who had decided to change public education by participating in it. One of the most exciting days of my young life involved taking the train to Albany to shout at the capitol building in a demonstration for school funding. (That, and the day I stole enough quarters from my parents' laundry stash to buy packs of Now-N-Later candies in every single flavor.)

I suppose that the notion of crunchy baked chicken began as an attempt to make low-fat fried chicken, but that was never a primary concern in my mother's kitchen. So she used dark meat, and dipped the chicken in half-and-half to make the cornflakes adhere in a most satisfying way.

½ to ¾ cup half-and-half

4 cups cornflakes

2 teaspoons dried rosemary

1 teaspoon garlic salt

⅛ teaspoon cayenne pepper
Salt and freshly ground black
  pepper
6 tablespoons unsalted butter,
  melted

4 pounds chicken legs and thighs,
  skinless

Preheat the oven to 375 degrees.

Pour the half-and-half into a shallow bowl. Lightly crush the cornflakes in another shallow bowl, and toss with the rosemary, garlic salt, cayenne, 1 teaspoon salt, and ½ teaspoon pepper.

Put 3 tablespoons of the melted butter in a large baking dish or pan.

Dip each piece of chicken in half-and-half and then the cornflake mixture. Repeat if necessary to build a crust that covers all the chicken, and put in the baking dish.

Sprinkle the whole dish with salt and pepper and drizzle with the remaining 3 tablespoons melted butter. Bake for 40 to 45 minutes, until the chicken is cooked through, crisp, and browned.

Makes 8 to 10 servings

NOT MY GRANDMOTHER'S BRISKET

My grandmother had many sterling qualities, but patience in the kitchen was not among them. Brisket was exactly the kind of slow-cooked dish she'd try to move along by turning up the heat: stiff gray meat was the inevitable result.

So, this brisket is my variation on a classic recipe by Nach Waxman, an old family friend who happened to open a cookbook store, Kitchen Arts & Letters, when I was in high school. My mother and I both worked there part-time, and our shared habit of cookbook acquisition began as soon as the employee discount kicked in. Nach was instrumental in getting me up to speed as a food writer.

Brisket may be the only American-ethnic classic that hasn't yet been gentrified, dolled up, or rediscovered by restaurant chefs. I've been served fancy matzo ball soup (with matzo balls in three different colors), "gourmet" tamales, and even a deconstructed Jamaican beef patty (that one was delicious). But brisket defies gentrification. As far as I can tell, the distinctive feature of brisket, as opposed to an Italian stracotto or French daube, is that there is no wine in the pot. (That, of course, is typical of the Jewish cooking of Eastern Europe, not exactly wine country.) But a huge quantity of caramelized onions, some paprika, and chicken broth do compensate.

One 8- to 10-pound beef brisket	1 tablespoon paprika
1 to 2 teaspoons all-purpose flour	1 cup chicken broth
Freshly ground black pepper	2 tablespoons tomato paste
¼ cup corn oil	1½ teaspoons kosher salt
8 onions, thickly sliced and	2 garlic cloves, quartered
separated into rings	1 carrot, peeled

Position a rack in the middle of the oven and preheat the oven to 375 degrees.

Trim the brisket of most of its fat. Dust it very lightly with the flour and sprinkle with pepper.

Heat the oil in a large heavy casserole over medium-high heat. Add the brisket and brown on both sides until some crisp spots appear on the surface. Transfer the brisket to a shallow dish or pan.

Keeping the heat at medium-high, add the onions to the casserole and stir, scraping up the brown particles left from the meat. Cook until the onions have softened and developed a handsome brown color, 10 to 15 minutes. Stir in the paprika and add the broth to the pot.

Remove the casserole from the heat and place the brisket, along with any juices that have accumulated, on top of the onions. Spread the tomato paste over the brisket (as if you were icing a cake). Sprinkle with pepper and the salt. Add the garlic and carrot to the pot and cover tightly. Transfer the casserole to the oven and cook for 1½ hours.

Remove the casserole from the oven and transfer the meat to a carving board. Cut it against the grain into ¼-inch-thick slices. Return the slices to the pot, overlapping them at an angle so that you can see a bit of the top edge of each slice (in effect, reassembling the brisket on a slight slant).

Cover, return the casserole to the oven, and cook for 1¾ to 2 hours longer, until the meat is fork-tender.

Remove the casserole from the oven and slice the carrot. Transfer the roast, onions, juices, and carrot slices to a heated platter. Serve immediately.

Makes 8 to 10 servings

BABY CARROTS WITH BLACK OLIVES

My mother gets upset about baby carrots, supersweet corn, and other agricultural innovations that favor appearance over flavor, but even she likes this dish. To save time, I make it with packaged baby carrots, which aren't "baby" at all but overgrown carrots whittled down to size. I think they are fine when cooked. She would use the real thing: sweet, immature carrots with the tops still attached. This recipe is adapted from Patricia Wells, the chic-est of my culinary surrogate mothers.

3 tablespoons extra-virgin
   olive oil
2 pounds baby carrots, halved on
   a diagonal
8 garlic cloves, slivered
Salt
30 oil-cured black olives, such as
   Nyons, pitted
A handful of chopped fresh
   parsley

Heat the oil over medium-high heat in a large skillet with a lid. When it ripples, add the carrots, stir to coat, and lower the heat to a moderate sizzle. Cover and cook for 10 minutes, stirring often.

Uncover the pan, add the garlic, and stir. Sprinkle with salt, reduce the heat to low, cover, and cook until the garlic is soft, another 15 minutes or so.

Stir in the olives and half the parsley and taste for salt. Transfer to a serving bowl, sprinkle with the remaining parsley, and serve hot or warm.

Makes 6 to 8 servings

LABOR-SAVING ORANGE CAKE

This fragrant cake is highly suitable for Mother's Day. It is also, I can attest, so easy that you can actually make it while becoming a mother. When I found myself zesting oranges and sifting flour during labor, I was astonished. Normally I take any excuse to lie around and read; I'd figured that labor would be one time I could take to my bed without apology. But it turns out that giving birth is, among other things, profoundly distracting. Reading was impossible; baking, with its step-by-step busywork, was just the ticket. And when we brought our son home just before his one-day birthday, we had a nice home-baked cake to put the candle on.

The cake is delicious made with fresh tangerine juice, but I usually use supermarket orange juice, and it always tastes swell. Do not even think about skipping the glaze; it is not a mere schmear for the top, but a juicy essence that soaks in to create a moist cake. This recipe is from Gale Gand, one of the best pastry chefs I've ever known and an inspiringly hardworking mother of three.

Finely grated zest of 3 oranges
3 tablespoons fresh orange juice
1 tablespoon fresh lemon juice
3 cups all-purpose flour, sifted
½ teaspoon baking soda
½ teaspoon salt

½ pound (2 sticks) unsalted
   butter, at room temperature
2 cups sugar
3 large eggs
1 cup buttermilk

FOR THE GLAZE
½ cup fresh orange juice
1 tablespoon fresh lemon juice

⅓ cup sugar

To make the cake: Preheat the oven to 350 degrees.

Butter a 9-inch round cake pan and line the bottom with parchment or waxed paper.

Stir the orange zest, orange juice, and lemon juice together. Sift the flour, baking soda, and salt together.

In the bowl of a stand mixer fitted with the paddle attachment, cream the butter until fluffy and light. Add the sugar and cream together. Add the eggs one at a time, mixing well after each addition.

With the mixer running at low speed, add the dry ingredients and the buttermilk in alternating batches, mixing until just combined. Add the juice mixture and mix.

Pour the batter into the prepared pan. Bake for 1 to 1¼ hours, until firm on top and a tester inserted into the center comes out clean (a few crumbs are OK). Let cool in the pan for 15 minutes.

To make the glaze: Meanwhile, make the glaze: Stir the juices and sugar together in a small bowl until the sugar dissolves.

Turn the warm cake out onto a wire rack set on a rimmed baking sheet (run a knife around the edges if it sticks at first). Peel off the paper. Use a baster or a brush to brush the glaze over the top. Let each addition soak in before adding more. Use all the glaze, including any that drips onto the baking sheet. Let cool to room temperature.

Serve the cake, or wrap well in plastic and refrigerate. Serve at room temperature or cold, in thin slices.

Makes one 9-inch cake

JUNE

THE VEGETARIAN CHALLENGE

JUNE
THE VEGETARIAN CHALLENGE

by **JULIA MOSKIN**

Some of my best friends are vegetarians, but as a tribe they stress me out. What with remembering who eats fish, and which couple is transitioning to vegan, and whether the children are allowed to have chicken nuggets, even the most mild-mannered vegetarians make high-maintenance guests.

However, their number is legion these days, and I can't argue with their logic. There is no way around the fact that the less meat we eat, the better: for the planet, for our health, for farms, for animals. Period. This is an uncomfortable truth for someone who loves a cheeseburger as much as I do. I can't possibly give up meat, but I would like to eat less of it.

The way this plays out in (hypocritical) practice is that I eat meat of all kinds when I'm not at home, even the "street meat" cooked on carts in midtown Manhattan. (The most delicious flesh food on earth, no doubt because it's pumped up on glutamates.) But when I'm shopping for my own kitchen, I won't buy meat or chicken or fish that has even a whiff of the feedlot or the battery cage. And so I quite often end up cooking vegetarian dinners, since the urge to pay $23 for an organic chicken that barely feeds a family of four doesn't come over me very often.

Severson, having lived in vegetarian enclaves like Berkeley and Brooklyn's Park

Slope, is quite strict about who qualifies as a vegetarian. Eggs, she believes, are not vegetarian fare. Milk, if known to have been produced by cheerful cows, is permissible. Her belief is that true vegetarians stay away from animal products altogether. So when cooking for vegetarians, she annoyingly refuses to use the cheap-and-easy "early Moosewood" method that so many of us have found helpful: cover everything in sight with melted cheese.

And these days, vegetarians are too sophisticated to fall for that. Other strategies are in order. I find that my veg friends are tired of being served pasta and tofu, two food groups that they usually have already mastered for themselves. They don't like tempeh or cracked wheat loaf any more than the rest of us. All the poor things want is really good food that just happens to be cruelty-free, which these days is easy enough to provide.

Now, let's be honest: when it comes to dinner, not only vegetarians, but vegetables themselves are troublesome. Many recipes for vegetarian dishes try to distract from their lack of protein by assembling a jumble of ingredients—look, you can have green peppers AND red peppers! AND mushrooms! AND carrots!—that ends up taking hours to put together. When I have a luxurious afternoon to cook, all that washing, peeling, and chopping is fine, but on a weeknight, a single onion is about all I can contend with.

So I gravitate toward recipes that contain shortcuts to intense flavor: nuts, cheese, herbs, vinegar. I also look for satisfying textures: potatoes, avocados, chickpeas, olives, and eggplant are particularly toothsome. Indian and Italian are the cuisines that most often shape themselves to a vegetarian agenda. (I have often thought that I could easily be a vegetarian if I happened to be an Indian Brahmin: my birthright would include thousands of recipes with dazzling spices and textures, and unlimited kitchen help.) I serve a lot of excellent bread and always something chocolate for dessert. Depending on how much you want to stuff people, any three of these dishes would suffice as a lovely simple dinner, and could be served all together. To really show off, serve each course separately, with slim, crunchy breadsticks.

SPICED NUTS WITH ROSEMARY

Nuts with a coating of rosemary, garlic, sugar, and cayenne: Sounds odd. Tastes amazing.

8 ounces raw almonds, walnuts, pecans, or cashews, or a combination

1 tablespoon finely chopped rosemary (fresh or dried)

¼ teaspoon cayenne pepper

1½ teaspoons light brown sugar

1 teaspoon salt

½ teaspoon very finely chopped garlic

½ teaspoon olive or walnut oil

Preheat the oven to 325 degrees.

Mix all the ingredients together and spread on a baking sheet, preferably lined with a nonstick baking mat or parchment paper. Bake for 10 minutes, then stir and bake 10 minutes more, or until golden and fragrant. Let cool on the pan.

Serve immediately, or store in an airtight container up to 1 week.

Makes 2 cups

MOZZARELLA, RED GRAPE, AND BLACK OLIVE SALAD

Juicy-crisp grapes are not considered as chefy as, say, melon or figs, but they have the advantage of always being in my refrigerator. I do not like grape desserts (having once been traumatized by a hot grape clafoutis), but in salads, they add the crunch of cucumber with the burstiness of tomatoes. In this recipe, which was adapted from Alice Waters via the London chef Sally Clarke, their sweetness plays nicely off the dry, wrinkled black olives. Note the technique of plunging the mozzarella into hot salted water to restore its just-made, drippy texture.

3 anchovy fillets (optional)

2 tablespoons sherry vinegar or balsamic vinegar

1 garlic clove, finely chopped

1 small dried red chile pepper or ½ teaspoon red pepper flakes

About ¾ cup oil-cured black olives, preferably Nyons, pitted

¼ cup extra-virgin olive oil, plus more for drizzling

8 ounces seedless red grapes, halved

1 small red onion, thinly sliced

A small handful of fresh parsley or cilantro leaves, plus extra for garnish

About 1 pound fresh mozzarella (large or small balls are fine)

Salt and freshly ground black pepper

Pound or chop together the anchovies, if using, vinegar, garlic, and chile until a rough paste forms. Mix with the olives and olive oil in a medium bowl and set aside for at least 30 minutes, or up to 4 hours.

Add the grapes, onion, and herbs to the olive mixture and gently toss together. Divide the mixture among serving plates.

When ready to serve, plunge the mozzarella into a bowl of hot salted water to warm it for 30 seconds, then drain.

Cut the mozzarella into slices or wedges and arrange on top of the olive salad. Drizzle with olive oil and sprinkle with salt and pepper. Sprinkle with herbs and serve.

Makes 4 to 6 servings

FRITTATA WITH CARAMELIZED ONIONS AND SHERRY VINEGAR

Deborah Madison, a goddess among vegetarians, cured me of a longtime fear of frittata. Like crème brûlée and mayonnaise until I'd made them, a frittata seemed rife with pitfalls: sticking, burning, falling. The best pan for frittata is a cast-iron skillet, set over very, very low heat, but you can use a nonstick pan. However, the first step of browning the onions can't be done in a nonstick pan, at least by me: they never brown properly and they do scorch.

2 tablespoons olive oil
1½ pounds onions, thinly sliced
2 tablespoons sherry vinegar
Pinch of freshly grated nutmeg
  (optional)
Salt and freshly ground black
  pepper

8 large eggs
2 tablespoons chopped fresh
  parsley, plus extra for garnish
2 tablespoons butter
½ cup walnut pieces, toasted
  (optional)

Heat the olive oil in a large skillet (preferably not nonstick) over medium heat. Add the onions and cook, stirring occasionally and adjusting the heat to make sure the onions sizzle steadily but do not brown too quickly or scorch. After about 30 minutes, they should be a limp, golden-brown tangle. Add 1 tablespoon of the vinegar, nutmeg, ¾ teaspoon salt, and pepper to taste, stir, and turn off the heat. Set aside at room temperature.

When almost ready to serve, preheat the broiler. Whisk the eggs with the parsley and a few pinches of salt in a large bowl. Mix in the onion mixture.

Melt 1 tablespoon of the butter in a 10-inch cast-iron or ovenproof nonstick skillet over low heat. Add the egg mixture, making sure the onions are evenly distributed in the pan. Scatter the walnuts on top, if using, and cook over very low heat until the frittata is set and golden brown on the bottom, about 10 minutes.

Slide the pan under the broiler (at least 4 inches away from the flame, to pre-

vent burning the walnuts) to finish cooking the top, about 2 minutes. Using a rubber spatula, loosen the frittata and slide it onto a serving plate.

Return the pan to the stove and melt the remaining tablespoon of butter. When it foams, add the remaining tablespoon of vinegar and swirl them together in the pan until hot. Pour over the frittata, garnish with parsley, and serve immediately, cut into wedges.

Makes 4 servings

PASTA E FAGIOLI

This soup illustrates the principle of "cook what you know": even basics like carrots, celery, and potatoes can appear new and different when combined in fresh ways. Inviting vegetarians to dinner should not make you feel pressured to experiment with broccolini and bok choy, if those are outside your kitchen-comfort zone. The basics, elevated, are good enough for anyone.

The combination of potatoes and pasta makes this dish silky and satisfying. Like most of the soups I make, this doesn't require any stock: water and just enough salt give it the right flavor. But it would not hurt to have a vegetable bouillon cube at hand in case of an attack of blandness: chile oil helps with that too.

¼ cup extra-virgin olive oil
1 onion, chopped
2 large carrots, chopped
2 large celery stalks, chopped
3 garlic cloves, minced
Kosher salt
2 bay leaves
¼ cup chopped fresh flat-leaf
  parsley, plus extra for garnish
10 fresh sage leaves, shredded

One 14-ounce can cannellini
  or borlotti beans, with their
  liquid
1 cup mashed potatoes
6 ounces fresh fettuccine, torn
  into 1-inch pieces
Freshly ground black pepper
Toasted Chile Oil (recipe follows)
  for drizzling
Parmesan cheese

Heat the oil in a soup pot over medium heat and add the onion, carrots, celery, garlic, 1 teaspoon salt, and the bay leaves and sauté, stirring often, until the vegetables are golden, about 10 minutes; adjust the heat as necessary to prevent browning.

Stir in the parsley and sage. Add the beans, with their liquid (rinse out the can with a little water to get all the starch), then add enough water to cover the ingredients by 2 inches. Add 1 teaspoon salt and the mashed potatoes and bring to a simmer. Add the pasta and cook, stirring often, until tender, about 3 minutes. Remove the bay leaves. Taste and season with salt and pepper. If the soup is too thick, thin with water and taste again for seasoning.

Ladle into shallow soup bowls, sprinkle with chopped parsley, and drizzle with chile oil and Parmesan cheese.

Makes about 6 servings

Toasted Chile Oil

I adapted this formula from the late chef Barbara Tropp, who educated so many Americans about real Chinese cooking with her book and San Francisco restaurant, both called China Moon. It yields a fragrant, fiery oil and a brick-red chile "sludge," both of which will keep indefinitely. They work as well in a wok as they do in the bean soup, or on top of a bowl of cold noodles.

⅔ cup red pepper flakes

4 garlic cloves, smashed and peeled

3 scallions, thinly sliced

2 tablespoons minced fresh ginger

2½ cups corn or peanut oil

⅓ cup roasted sesame oil

Combine all the ingredients in a large saucepan fitted with a deep-frying thermometer. Bring to 225 to 250 degrees over medium-low heat, stirring occasionally. Simmer for 15 minutes, checking the temperature often to make sure it does not rise above 250 degrees. Remove from the heat and let cool to room temperature.

Scrape the oil and solids into a glass or plastic container and store tightly covered at room temperature.

Makes about 3 cups

CHOCOLATE CHIFFON CAKE

Bakers tend to fetishize butter, but I think it muffles the taste of chocolate. Oil-based chocolate cakes have more character; this one was adapted from a classic recipe by Mary Bergin, the original pastry chef at Spago in Los Angeles. Serve with a sprinkling of confectioners' sugar, or a drizzle of cold cream.

¾ cup unsweetened cocoa
    powder, plus extra for
    the pans
1½ cups sugar
1 cup all-purpose flour
2 teaspoons baking powder
1 teaspoon baking soda
¼ teaspoon salt
4 large eggs, separated
¾ cup vegetable oil
½ cup water
1 teaspoon vanilla extract
2 large egg whites

Position a rack in the center of the oven and preheat the oven to 350 degrees. Butter two 9-inch round cake pans or spray with nonstick spray. Dust with cocoa powder, tapping out any excess.

Sift together 1 cup of the sugar, the flour, cocoa, baking powder, baking soda, and salt. Set aside.

In the bowl of a stand mixer, beat the egg yolks at high speed. Turn the speed to low and slowly pour in the oil, water, and vanilla. Gradually add the sifted dry ingredients; when they are almost incorporated, turn the speed to medium and beat until well combined. Remove the bowl from the mixer. (Transfer the mixture to another bowl if you only have one mixer bowl.)

In a clean mixer bowl, with clean beaters, whip the 6 egg whites until soft peaks form, starting on medium speed and raising the speed as peaks begin to form.

Gradually pour in the remaining ½ cup sugar and whip until the whites are shiny and firm but not stiff.

With a rubber spatula, fold one-quarter of the whites into the chocolate mixture, then scrape the chocolate mixture into the remaining whites, quickly folding it in until completely incorporated.

Scrape the batter into the prepared pans. Bake for about 30 minutes, until the edges of the cake pull away from the pan and a tester gently inserted into the middle of a cake comes out clean. Cool in the pans on a rack for 15 minutes. Run a sharp knife around the inside of each pan to loosen the cake and invert onto a rack to cool completely. Once cool, the cakes can be wrapped tightly in plastic and refrigerated for up to three days. If serving only one layer, freeze the other.

Makes two 9-inch layers

THE VEGETARIAN CHALLENGE

by **KIM SEVERSON**

Despite all my politically correct street cred— years in Berkeley, more than one Michigan Womyn's Music Festival ticket stub, emotional scars from fighting to get The Man's foot off people's necks—I have sinned. I have mocked vegans. And I have put chicken stock in dishes I've fed to vegetarians. (In my defense, they commented that the dishes were very good. Surprisingly so, they said.)

Still, I feel bad. At the time, I was having difficulty figuring out how to recast the food I like to make do without meat. And to make do without animal products altogether? Baffling.

After years of whipping up little batches of Marcella Hazan's simple, bright butter, onion, and tomato sauce to serve over pasta alongside my three-meat ragù, I began to see that it made more sense to cook for the vegetarians and vegans rather than around them.

This opened whole new arenas of kitchen exploration. Cooking for people who don't eat animal products is a challenge I try to embrace as a way to break out of my own rut. Grains are the go-to, but what a world to explore. Things have moved way beyond tabouli, my friends. We have quinoa, which can be a more nutritional answer to the rice of a risotto, but can take the same creamy treatment and marry spring vegetables like peas or favas or earthier fall flavors of mushrooms and squash.

In the South, where I now live, I learned simple tricks for vegetables that work well and save time, like grating raw sweet potato into grits before they cook and how to get the very best flavors out of field peas using other vegetables and aromatics from the garden.

And although Moskin cringes at having to deal with more than one vegetable at a time, a truly great vegetarian meal rises and falls on variety and thoughtful preparation.

But I have also learned, after all these years, that being a vegetarian or a vegan means something different to each one. People are flexitarians. Or they eat cheese but not milk. They have bacon exceptions.

So now, before I reach for the chicken stock, I ask. Often the answer is yes.

MINT AND CUCUMBER SODA

Since I don't drink alcohol anymore, I am always casting around for interesting drinks that aren't too sweet. These can be made in bigger batches, which is what you'll want to do, because everyone will want one, whether they drink alcohol or not.

4 ounces or a cup sliced peeled,
    English cucumber (if using
    regular cucumber, seed it
    as well)
¼ cup tightly packed fresh mint
    leaves
Juice of 2 limes
2 to 3 tablespoons minted agave
    syrup (see Note)
Seltzer or soda water

Using a wooden spoon or potato masher, mash the cucumber slices with the mint leaves, lime juice, and 2 tablespoons of the agave syrup until the cucumber is crushed. Cover and shake well to combine; then strain into two glasses filled to the top with ice. Top with seltzer to taste, and add more agave syrup if needed.

Makes 2 servings

Note: To make minted agave syrup, bring ½ cup agave syrup to a slow boil with ¼ bunch fresh mint. Remove from the heat and let steep for at least 30 minutes; strain. Leftover syrup will keep in the fridge for several weeks.

KALE CHIPS

I stole this trick from my former editor, Pete Wells, who is now the *New York Times* restaurant critic. He, I think, stole it from Jacques Pépin, who probably stole it from someone else. It is the best party trick ever.

1 bunch kale, preferably lacinato
2 tablespoons olive oil

Kosher or sea salt

Preheat the oven to 300 degrees.

Tear the kale leaves into 4 or 5 pieces each, removing big stems. Spread them out on a large rimmed baking sheet (trying not to overlap much), drizzle with the olive oil, and toss to coat. Sprinkle on about ½ teaspoon salt.

Bake for about 20 minutes, turning every so often. The kale will diminish in volume dramatically. Serve hot.

Makes a bowlful that might satisfy 4 people

FRESH PEA CROSTINI

These make the best use of fresh green peas, but they can be made with frozen peas when the season isn't right. Pea tendrils are often available at Asian markets or at farmers' markets in the spring.

FOR THE PUREE

1¼ cups fresh green peas (from 1½ pounds peas in pod)
1 cup chickpeas, rinsed
¼ cup chopped fresh flat-leaf parsley

¼ cup plain whole-milk yogurt
3 tablespoons chopped scallions
2 tablespoons fresh lemon juice
2 teaspoons ground cumin
¾ teaspoon salt

FOR THE TOASTS

25 thin baguette slices
2 tablespoons extra-virgin olive oil

Pea tendrils (optional)

To make the puree: Combine the peas, chickpeas, parsley, yogurt, scallions, lemon juice, cumin, and salt in a food processor and puree until almost smooth.

To make the toasts: Toast the bread in a 350 degree oven, brush the toasts with the olive oil, and top with the pea hummus. Garnish with pea tendrils, if desired.

Makes 25 crostini

FARRO SALAD

I made this once when I was a guest star in a video segment for Food52, the excellent website and recipe forum my colleague Amanda Hesser started with Merrill Stubbs. The recipe was contributed by Jennifer Perillo, and it gets its flavor from the way the farro is cooked and from an interesting dressing with two vinegars.

FOR THE SALAD

2 cups uncooked farro (or substitute barley)

1 medium red onion, cut in half

1 garlic clove

A handful of fresh parsley sprigs, plus 1 tablespoon finely chopped fresh parsley

½ teaspoon salt, plus more if needed

1 cup finely diced (about ¼-inch) fresh mozzarella cheese

2 teaspoons minced pitted Kalamata olives

1 pint grape tomatoes, cut into quarters

1 tablespoon finely chopped fresh basil

Freshly ground black pepper

FOR THE DRESSING

Scant ¼ cup extra-virgin olive oil

1 tablespoon red wine vinegar

1 teaspoon balsamic vinegar

2 teaspoons honey

To cook the farro: Combine the farro, 1 onion half, the garlic, handful of parsley, the salt, and 2¾ cups water in a 2-quart saucepan and bring to a boil, then cover, reduce to a simmer, and cook for 10 minutes. Turn off the heat and let sit, covered, for 5 minutes.

Discard the onion, garlic, and large sprigs of parsley. Spread the farro out on a rimmed baking sheet and let cool completely (do not skip this step, or the mozzarella will melt into the salad).

To make the dressing: Whisk together the olive oil, vinegars, and honey in a small bowl.

To assemble the salad: Finely chop the remaining onion half. Combine the onion, cooled farro, mozzarella, olives, tomatoes, the remaining tablespoon of parsley, and the basil in a deep bowl. Pour the dressing over the ingredients and stir well to combine, using a wooden spoon or rubber spatula. Season with salt and pepper to taste. The salad is ready to serve, but it can be made up to 1 day ahead and stored in the fridge, covered.

Makes 8 servings

CRISP MAPLE WAFERS

This recipe is adapted from that old standby, the *Joy of Cooking*. You can use some of the fine butter substitutes to make them vegan. These will seem thin at first, but don't worry.

½ cup maple syrup

4 tablespoons butter

¼ teaspoon vanilla extract

½ cup all-purpose flour, sifted

¼ teaspoon salt

Preheat the oven to 350 degrees. Line a baking sheet with a nonstick baking mat.

Combine the maple syrup, butter, and vanilla in a small saucepan, bring to a hard boil, and boil for 30 seconds. Remove from the heat and whisk in the flour and salt until the mixture is smooth and there are no lumps whatsoever.

Arrange tablespoons of the batter 2 to 3 inches apart on the lined baking sheet. Bake for 12 to 13 minutes, or until the cookies spread and take on a lace-like appearance. Let cool completely on the pan. Repeat with the remaining batter.

Makes about 15 cookies

THE PICNIC CHALLENGE

KIM'S MENU

Picnic Fried Chicken

Cucumber-Watermelon Salad

No-Mayo Potato Salad

Peach Cake

JULIA'S MENU

Green-Salad Soup

Bazargan (Cracked Wheat Salad with Pomegranate Dressing)

Pan Bagnat (Salade Niçoise Sandwich)

Strawberries with Homemade Ricotta and Demerara Sugar

Supernatural Brownies

THE PICNIC CHALLENGE

by **KIM SEVERSON**

This is America, I often have to remind Moskin. Sure, we've borrowed the culinary history of plenty of other countries. Hell, most of us are from somewhere else, if you think about it. But there are some things that have simply been so for so long that they are ours, clear and free. A picnic is one of them.

Eating outdoors is one of the great parts of our culinary fabric, starting with the clambake and moving through our expansion westward. The cowboy campfire meal, the pit barbecue, the salmon roast—all of them come from the great American tradition that is a meal eaten outdoors.

So leave it to Moskin to try to French it up with a pan bagnat. Most people planning a picnic don't even know how to pronounce it. What they want on a picnic is fried chicken. And that is what I offer here.

I have experienced a lot of food outdoors. There were soggy, cold ham sandwiches eaten on a seat in my father's fishing boat, which also doubled as a ski boat when he needed a way to keep five children entertained on the camping trips that were the only vacations we could afford. I've eaten many a hobo pack on Girl Scout outings, carefully cooking my little foil packet of ground beef and potatoes over a fire. There was the backpacking trip through the Denali wilderness, where

I'd stupidly brought a bottle of wine. The weight of the bottle (packed both in and out) was a rookie mistake.

Through it all, I have learned that what you pack matters, in terms of both food and equipment. Even on the shortest walks from car to picnic grounds, food will jostle. Dressing will leak. Dishes that need to stay cool will get warm. That's why a good spread must be built from sturdy food.

The other essential ingredient is what you sit on. If you think through nothing else, think through this: that picnic blanket matters. I have found one with a strong synthetic backing that keeps moisture from seeping up and provides a nice bit of padding. You can get fancy and throw a tablecloth over it, if you like. But no one is going to enjoy their food crammed onto a little corner of that old thin blanket you picked up when you went to Mexico on spring break.

Now, let me pause here for a moment and ask you to really think about that mayonnaise. Because it is made with eggs, the USDA and restaurant inspectors caution against leaving it at room temperature for too long. That is not why I caution against it. I caution against it because it rarely adds anything to a picnic. And, if we are telling the truth here, I can't stand the commercial version that most people use. I can only handle homemade mayonnaise and its cousin, aioli. And even if someone goes to the trouble to make it, I still think it has no place on a picnic spread.

But I'll tell you what does: fried chicken, it's the perfect and quintessential American picnic food. Paired with a cool and chunky salad of watermelon and cucumber and a potato salad that is bright with vinegar (of course, no mayo), you've got a perfect meal.

But the real showstopper is the peach cake. The one-layer cake is not hard to pack for a picnic, as long as you wrap it well in waxed paper and then plenty of foil to protect it. A large round plastic container is good too. Avoid packing it in slices if you can—it ruins the lovely effect pulling a whole cake from the basket will have on your picnic mates.

No fancy French tuna sandwich can do that.

PICNIC FRIED CHICKEN

This was inspired by my mother's recipe, mixed with the good fried chicken I have eaten in the South. My mother taught me to season the flour with a little heat from cayenne and shake it all in a paper bag. Another trick is to add cornstarch to the flour mixture to help it adhere. And another is to remove the chicken from the hot oil with tongs, holding the piece sideways over the pan to let the fat drip off more completely.

Consider making a little more than you think you need. And make sure to cut the breasts crosswise in half using a heavy knife or cleaver. That way, you'll have plenty for everyone.

¼ cup plus 1 teaspoon kosher salt
1 quart buttermilk
One 3-pound chicken, cut into
  8 pieces (see the headnote)
1 cup all-purpose flour
2 tablespoons cornstarch

4 teaspoons cayenne pepper
½ teaspoon freshly ground black
  pepper
2 cups canola or peanut oil

Stir the ¼ cup salt into the buttermilk. Put the chicken in a large bowl or dish and cover with the buttermilk. Cover with plastic wrap and refrigerate for 6 to 8 hours, or overnight.

Drain the chicken well. Put the flour, cornstarch, remaining teaspoon of salt, the cayenne, and black pepper in a brown paper bag and shake to combine the spices. Add the chicken pieces a few at a time and shake well to coat. Place chicken pieces on a plate and prepare to fry.

Heat the oil in a cast-iron skillet over medium-high heat to about 330 degrees. Slip the chicken in a few pieces at a time, skin side down; do not crowd the chicken. (You might want to use two pans to speed things along.) Turn the heat down a bit to medium and cook for 10 minutes, then flip the chicken. Continue cooking until the chicken is done, about another 10 minutes. Drain on a wire rack or on crumpled paper towels or newspaper.

Makes 8 pieces

CUCUMBER-WATERMELON SALAD

I've been tweaking this salad for years. Sometimes I use different peppers for heat, but I keep coming back to jalapeños, which bring something vegetal along with the heat. I've tried both pine nuts and almonds, but I think the pistachios add an unexpected note. The lime juice offsets the sweetness of the hoisin, and the whole thing just gets better with a little time to meld. Pack this on some ice. It's best cool.

4 cups generous ½-inch cubes seeded watermelon

3 cups ½-inch pieces peeled seeded Asian or English cucumbers (about 2 large cucumbers)

3½ tablespoons fresh lime juice

3 tablespoons hoisin sauce

2 teaspoons finely diced seeded jalapeño, or to taste

½ teaspoon salt

⅓ cup chopped fresh flat-leaf parsley

Freshly ground black pepper

⅓ cup coarsely chopped lightly salted pistachios

Combine the watermelon and cucumbers in a colander and set over a medium bowl. Cover with plastic wrap and refrigerate for at least 30 minutes, or up to 4 hours.

Discard the liquid, and put the watermelon and cucumbers in a serving bowl.

Whisk the lime juice, hoisin, jalapeño, and salt in a small bowl. Pour over the watermelon and cucumbers. Add the parsley and toss gently. Add a few grinds of black pepper.

When you are ready to serve, sprinkle the salad with the pistachios.

Makes about 7 cups, or 6 to 8 servings

NO-MAYO POTATO SALAD

This salad gets better with time. It's perfect if you make it in the morning and let it sit at room temperature until it's time for your picnic. Make sure the potatoes are well cooked but not overcooked, or they will fall apart.

2 pounds small potatoes,
    preferably a mix of colors
3 slices bacon
1 tablespoon grainy mustard
¼ cup red wine vinegar
1 teaspoon salt, or more to taste

½ teaspoon freshly ground black
    pepper, or more to taste
½ cup olive oil
4 scallions, thinly sliced
¼ cup chopped flat-leaf parsley

Boil the potatoes in a large pot of salted water until tender, about 20 minutes. Drain and place in a large bowl to cool slightly.

Meanwhile, fry the bacon until crisp. Drain on paper towels. Crumble and set aside.

Whisk the mustard, vinegar, salt, and pepper in a small bowl. Slowly drizzle in the olive oil, whisking constantly.

Toss the potatoes with the dressing and let cool to room temperature.

Add the bacon, scallions, and parsley to the potatoes and toss. Taste and adjust for salt and pepper if necessary.

Makes 6 servings

PEACH CAKE

This was inspired by Marian Burros, a longtime Dining writer at the *Times* and a mentor of sorts to both Julia and me. She made a plum torte that became one of the paper's most-requested recipes ever. Some years later, former *Times* Dining writer Amanda Hesser started a community cooking website called Food52 that has a version of a plum cake that built on the plum torte. My cake uses peaches, which are a bit juicier and make for a cake that can stand on its own without whipped cream, which is a pain to take on a picnic. (Though if you make this for non-picnic purposes, by all means serve it warm with whipped cream, stabilized with a little yogurt or crème fraîche stirred in.)

8 tablespoons (1 stick) unsalted
  butter, at room temperature,
  plus more for the pan
1½ cups unbleached all-purpose
  flour
1 teaspoon baking powder
¼ teaspoon baking soda
½ teaspoon kosher salt
⅔ cup granulated sugar
2 large eggs, at room temperature
¾ cup sour cream, at room
  temperature
½ teaspoon vanilla extract
½ teaspoon grated lime zest

2 tablespoons dark brown sugar
8 medium peaches, pitted and
  quartered

Position a rack in the lower third of the oven and preheat the oven to 350 degrees. Butter a 9-inch round cake pan, line it with parchment, and butter the parchment. Dust the pan with flour, tapping out the excess.

Whisk together the flour, baking powder, baking soda, and salt in a small bowl. Set aside.

In the bowl of a stand mixer fitted with the paddle attachment (or in a large bowl, using a handheld mixer), beat together the butter and granulated sugar on

medium speed until light and fluffy, about 5 minutes. Mix in the eggs one at a time, beating well and scraping down the bowl after each addition. Mix in the sour cream, vanilla, and lime zest. On low speed, add the flour mixture, mixing just until combined. The batter will be thick.

With a rubber spatula, spread half of the batter evenly in the bottom of the prepared pan. Sprinkle with 1 tablespoon of the brown sugar and top with half the peach wedges, set on their sides. Spread the rest of the batter over the peaches, trying not to disturb them. Arrange the rest of the peaches on top and sprinkle with the remaining tablespoon of brown sugar. Bake for about 50 minutes, or until the cake is golden and a toothpick inserted near the center comes out clean. Cool on a rack for 30 minutes or so.

Run a thin knife around the inside of the pan to loosen the cake. Cover the top with a large plate, then flip the cake over so it slips nicely onto the plate. Peel off the parchment. Then flip the cake again onto a serving plate; or, flip it into a plastic container for carrying it to the picnic, or onto a foil-covered piece of sturdy cardboard, and cover with more foil for transport.

Makes 8 servings, or 6 if you really like peach cake

THE PICNIC CHALLENGE

by JULIA MOSKIN

When I told Severson that I was thinking about doing a French sandwich and a Middle Eastern salad for my picnic menu, she looked at me politely. This is always a bad sign. I could tell that having already staked out fried chicken and potato salad for her menu, she was not feeling threatened. At heart, she believes that I am an East Coast food snob and that she is the true taste of the heartland.

Let me tell you something about Severson: she's a mayonnaise snob. And, having lived in northern California, she is also a salad snob.

The question of food snobbery comes up a lot in our line of work, as in "Oh, you must be a *food snob*." I'm taking this opportunity to declare the term meaningless—and also to embrace it. It is not snobbery to care about the way food tastes: everyone does. And everyone makes food choices based on a complex algorithm of appetite, money, and morality. I'll eat New York City street hot dogs, but not a Starbucks scone—ever. I feed my kids frozen tater tots but don't allow chocolate chip pancakes. Everyone has preferences in food, and as long as they are honest, the world is a more interesting place for it.

So, let us bring our snobberies to light. Mine include a loathing of paper plates and plastic forks. And I am not ashamed to say that I love fancy restaurants, with the sparkling glasses, the graceful heavy silverware, the plates that are brought to me by waiters and, later, washed and put away by someone who is not me.

Picnics are the opposite of all that. I love them anyway, but I have developed a picnic menu that suits my rules. Almost all the food is meant to be handheld: olives, mozzarella balls, cherry tomatoes, cookies, and a big sandwich cut into manageable chunks. This is usually a pan bagnat, a compressed mass of tuna, sliced eggs, tomatoes, and black olives, all saturated with lashings of golden olive oil. (You can wipe your hands on the grass, or rinse them in the ocean.)

I met and married this sandwich at the age of thirteen. The pan bagnat, essentially a salade Niçoise in a loaf of bread, was the only snack available at the municipal swimming pool in northern Provence, where my family spent that summer. The previous year, we had traveled to Greece on airplane tickets that turned out to be stolen and shared a two-room house on a speck of an island with a toothless black-clad widow. (It had not occurred to her that renting out her house would mean leaving it; she just moved her bed into the kitchen.) I had looked forward to visiting a country where I believed that no one would try to squeeze goat's milk into my mouth (this happened somewhere between Athens and the Peloponnesian islands).

But my parents' version of the South of France—nowhere near the ocean, filled with boring (to me) lavender distilleries—drove me and my sister to restless madness. One day, we loaded up a quaint wicker basket and drove to Avignon; when my father shouldered the basket, the jug of olive oil tipped over and soaked his shirt.

Despite these setbacks, my parents continued to insist on picnics while traveling. By the end of a six-week-long driving odyssey in Eastern Europe in 1987, we were reduced to stopping on ever-more-windblown off-ramps of Polish highways, eating pickled mushrooms we'd bought weeks earlier in Germany right out of the jar.

Perhaps this explains why planning a picnic can keep me up on a summer night.

At the bare minimum, and a very filling minimum it is too, a few cheeses, salami, and the "crusty bread" that food writers are forever recommending make an estimable picnic, leaving more time for the scavenger hunt or lake swim. Bring a bag of cherries, promise an ice cream stop on the way home, and call it good.

GREEN-SALAD SOUP

Although I can't quite believe it, I have been told that there are people out there who get tired of green salad. I am always happy to consume something so lively, fast, and inarguably healthy. For a picnic, tossed salad is impractical, but this soup is cool, green, and delicious. It is adapted from the vegetable genius Yotam Ottolenghi, a chef in London.

2 celery stalks with leaves
2 small green bell peppers, cored
  and seeded
1¼ pounds cucumbers, peeled,
  halved lengthwise, and seeded
  (about 1½ large)
3 slices stale white bread, crusts
  removed
4 garlic cloves
1 teaspoon sugar
4 ounces baby spinach

1 cup loosely packed fresh basil
  leaves
2 tablespoons chopped fresh
  parsley
¼ cup sherry vinegar, or more
  to taste
1 cup olive oil
3 tablespoons Greek yogurt
2 teaspoons salt, or more to taste

Roughly chop the celery, bell peppers, cucumbers, bread, and garlic together. Working in batches, puree them in a blender, loosening the mixture with trickles of cold water as needed. When all of the vegetables have been pureed, return the entire mixture to the blender and add the remaining ingredients, pulsing as you go, until everything is smooth and incorporated. Add a handful of ice cubes and blend. Taste and adjust the seasonings with salt and vinegar.

Just before serving, add more ice and pulse once or twice, until crushed. Or, for a picnic, take the soup along in a Thermos, and serve over ice cubes.

Makes 6 to 8 servings

BAZARGAN
(CRACKED WHEAT SALAD
WITH POMEGRANATE DRESSING)

This Middle Eastern whole-grain salad is complex enough to transform a pick-up picnic of cheese, salami, and tomatoes into a Mediterranean feast. It is related to tabouli but far more interesting and savory. In Arabic, its name means something along the lines of "everything from the bazaar," meaning that it's assembled from pantry ingredients. Aleppo chile, toasted and rich, is a Syrian staple. My friend Lisa, one of the best cooks I know, introduced me to bazargan.

1 pound bulgur, preferably
  medium or coarse
4 cups vegetable or tomato
  juice, chilled

FOR THE DRESSING
½ cup extra-virgin olive oil
3 tablespoons pomegranate
  molasses, or more to taste
2 teaspoons ground toasted
  cumin seeds (or use 1 teaspoon
  ground cumin from a jar)
2 teaspoons ground coriander
½ teaspoon ground allspice
Cayenne or Aleppo chile pepper
Juice of 1 lemon, or more to taste
Salt and freshly ground black
  pepper

2 cups toasted pine nuts or
  walnuts, or a combination,
  coarsely chopped

1 cup finely chopped fresh
  flat-leaf parsley or mint, or a
  combination
½ cup thinly sliced scallions
  (optional)

At least a few hours or up to a day before serving, put the bulgur in a large bowl and pour in the vegetable juice. Mix, and refrigerate until the wheat completely absorbs the juice and begins to soften, about 30 minutes. Add 2 cups lightly salted cold water and refrigerate again. Repeat the process until the bulgur is tender but still firm: it will become softer later when it absorbs the dressing. Drain in a sieve.

To make the dressing: Whisk the oil, molasses, cumin, coriander, allspice, a large pinch of chile pepper, and the lemon juice together in a bowl (or combine in a jar and shake well). Add salt and pepper, then taste and adjust the seasonings with salt and lemon juice: It should have sweet-tart notes from the molasses (add more as needed) but be warm and earthy from the spices.

Pour the dressing over the bulgur and mix very well. Refrigerate until ready to serve.

Just before serving, add the nuts, herbs, and scallions, if using, and mix well.

Makes 8 to 10 servings

PAN BAGNAT
(SALADE NIÇOISE SANDWICH)

In the year of my thirteenth summer, my parents took my sister and me to the south of France. That sounds glamorous, but our small house in a town far inland came with scorpions, rocks, and nowhere to swim. Blazing heat drove us to the local municipal swimming pool every day, where there still was nothing to do, but at least we could watch the local boys see how close to the side of the pool they could dive without hitting it, and eat pan bagnat. These were assembled each morning and left to marinate at *le snack bar*, melding the flavors and textures in a way that I still consider the hallmark of a good sandwich. (Some foolish people call it "soggy.")

¼ cup pitted green olives,
    preferably Picholine
1 garlic clove, smashed and
    peeled
Olive oil
1 large loaf peasant-style bread
    with a chewy crust

Two 6-ounce cans tuna packed in
    olive oil, drained
3 or 4 hard-boiled eggs, thinly
    sliced (optional)
3 ripe tomatoes, sliced
Fresh basil leaves
Freshly ground black pepper

Coarsely chop the olives and garlic together. Transfer to a small bowl and add olive oil to cover.

To assemble the sandwich: Cut the bread horizontally in half. Using a pastry brush dipped in the olive-garlic mixture, paint the cut sides of the bread with oil.

Flake the tuna with a fork and distribute it over the bottom half of the bread. Cover with slices of egg, if using. Cover the egg with slices of tomato. Spoon the olive-garlic mixture evenly over the tomatoes. Cover with basil leaves. Grind black pepper on top and cover with the top half of the bread.

Wrap the sandwich tightly in parchment or waxed paper. Place a heavy skillet on top to slowly compress the sandwich, and refrigerate for at least 1 hour, or up to 3 hours. Use a large serrated knife to cut the sandwich into wedges or slices.

Makes 6 to 8 servings

STRAWBERRIES WITH HOMEMADE RICOTTA AND DEMERARA SUGAR

Lovers of Greek yogurt, crème fraîche, and plain old sour cream will never look back after making ricotta at home with this technique: apply heat and little bit of acid to milk—whether grass-fed, organic, or supermarket—and it will separate with startling obedience into curds and whey. The "cheese maker" has only to stand there with a ladle, or colander, and some cheesecloth. A fifteen-minute wait produces fluffy ricotta with a fresh milky flavor that no amount of cash can buy. It's perfect with summer fruit.

FOR THE RICOTTA
2 quarts whole milk
2 cups buttermilk

Ripe strawberries (or other ripe berries in season)
Demerara or Muscovado sugar (or regular brown sugar)

To make the ricotta: Line a wide colander with cheesecloth, folded so that it is at least 4 layers thick. Place it in the sink.

Pour the milk and buttermilk into a heavy pot, and attach a candy thermometer. Heat over high heat, stirring frequently and scraping the bottom of the pot occasionally to prevent scorching. As the milk heats, curds will begin to rise and clump on the surface. Once the mixture is steaming hot, stop stirring. When the mixture reaches 175 to 180 degrees on the candy thermometer, curds and whey will separate. (The whey will look like cloudy gray water underneath the mass of thick white curds.) Immediately turn off the heat and gently ladle the curds into the colander.

When the dripping from the curds has slowed, about 5 minutes, gently gather the edges of the cheesecloth and twist to bring the curds together; do not squeeze. Let drain for 15 minutes more.

Untie the cloth and pack the ricotta into airtight containers. Keep refrigerated. This will last about two days.

If serving picnic-style, let each person dip berries into the ricotta and then into the sugar (bring the sugar in a container or a twist of parchment paper). Alternatively, spoon the ricotta into small bowls and top with berries and sugar.

Makes about 2 cups ricotta (can be doubled)

SUPERNATURAL BROWNIES

Whether your brownie sits on the fudgy or the cakey side of the aisle, its character should come from the underlying structure of flour, sugar, butter, eggs, and chocolate, not from frills like marshmallows or peanut butter. This perfect formula is the accidental creation of baking guru Nick Malgieri, who (in a rare human moment for a pastry chef) once forgot to double the flour when baking his own fudge brownie recipe. He also adds a measure of brown sugar.

½ pound (2 sticks) unsalted butter, cut into chunks, plus more for the pan

8 ounces bittersweet chocolate, coarsely chopped

4 large eggs

½ teaspoon salt

1 cup granulated sugar

1 cup packed dark brown sugar, such as Muscovado

2 teaspoons vanilla extract

1 cup all-purpose flour

½ cup chopped walnuts or ¾ cup whole walnuts (optional)

Preheat the oven to 350 degrees. Butter a 13-by-9-inch baking pan, line with parchment paper, and butter the paper.

Melt the butter and chocolate together in the top of a double boiler over barely simmering water, or on low power in a microwave. Let cool slightly.

Whisk the eggs together in a large bowl (or use a stand mixer). Whisk in the salt, sugars, and vanilla. Whisk in the chocolate mixture. Fold in the flour just until combined. If using chopped (not whole) walnuts, stir them in.

Pour the batter into the prepared pan. If using whole walnuts, arrange on top of batter. Bake for 35 to 40 minutes, or until the brownies are shiny and beginning to crack on top. Cool completely in the pan on a rack.

Serve, or, for best flavor, store, tightly wrapped, overnight before serving.

Makes 2 dozen brownies

HEIRLOOM TOMATOES

AUGUST

THE FARMERS' MARKET CHALLENGE

THE FARMERS' MARKET CHALLENGE

by JULIA MOSKIN

Although Manhattan is my native habitat, and although Severson finds it hilarious to paint me as a pampered city girl in heels, a lot of my childhood was spent in Upstate New York, in a scruffy region about two hours north of the city. (Also, I never wear heels. Ask anyone.)

Columbia County is a hilly, rocky county wedged between the Hudson River and the Berkshires. It's not quaint or manicured, just family farm country like anywhere else in America until the 1950s. The county was once a major supplier of milk to the big city a hundred miles south, but those dairy farms were already fading when I was young and disappeared entirely during the 1980s. Until a few years ago, the main salad greens at the local A&P were iceberg lettuce and red cabbage. Over the last twenty years it's been a long, slow road back to farming here, with many small growers of greens, tomatoes, and herbs taking root alongside established apple orchards and commercial farms.

In the 1970s, my hippieish (and food-obsessed) parents earnestly tried to interest us in gardening during the summers spent up there. Their efforts produced an annual flood of tomatoes and not much else; we'd buy produce direct from the local dairy farmers, who often cultivated an acre or so of vegetables alongside their cows. I loved (and still do) the summer sports of watching and waiting for the

corn to ripen and making gallons of tomato sauce at the end of the summer. Julia Child isn't exactly known for tomato sauce, but her orange-and-coriander-scented version is my family's summer prize. (In her book, it's called Coulis de Tomatoes à la Provençale, which might explain why no one ever seems to make it.) We make a huge quantity over Labor Day weekend, when bushels of not-so-pretty but superripe tomatoes go on sale at the farmstands.

But in my daily life, obsessing over fresh local produce—not to mention sustainable and organic—isn't natural to me. Unlike Severson, I haven't ever lived in a perfect-produce bubble like Berkeley, California, nor am I descended from Midwestern farmers. (In fact, her fantastic scalloped tomatoes—like a combination of pizza and bread pudding—are the first ones I ever tried.) And now, as a working mother of two, I find cooking itself hard enough without the added pressure of "seasonality." But when August comes around with its irresistible flood of beans, corn, tomatoes, zucchini, and all those things that make dinner simple—grilled steak or fish or burgers—I jump in. To be honest, it's the one time of the year when I really do cook seasonally and locally.

My first grilling experiences were not promising. As a young thing about town, I'd sometimes invite friends up to the country for Saturday night and serve them charred chicken, red at the bone, or rubberized steaks. Traumatized by this, I developed a mantra: "Sausages: they never overcook." Although that is patently untrue, it was an easy out, and I served many dry, gnarled specimens alongside spectacular local produce.

The problem with my approach to grilling, it turns out, is that it was too fancy.

I could not resist marinating and rubbing and studding and all the other things you can do to a steak. These days, since steak is no longer something most of us eat weekly, the basic flavors of meat, salt, and blood are exciting enough. I find the texture of skirt steak, a thrifty cut, far superior to the overworked flank. Char the heck out of it, let it rest, and save your energy for making corn fritters.

What can compete with corn fritters, Ms. Severson? Nothing, really, especially when there is a pool of maple syrup for dipping. Of course, oil-frying is not the first activity that comes to mind on a hot summer day. But in the cool of a Labor Day weekend, when the corn is as high as a city-girl's eye, the sweat is well worth it.

JULIA CHILD'S TOMATO SAUCE

I'm willing to admit that the Severson's family tomato sauce is the last word in Italian-American cooking. She's a solid fifty-percent Italian, and I'm a hundred-percent Jewish. What do I know about tomato sauce? Well, I wasn't named after Julia Child for nothing. This meatless sauce, adapted from *Mastering the Art of French Cooking*, stands on its own: the orange peel and coriander seed give it a sunny Mediterranean flavor. In January, thawing out a quart of it is like arriving at the beach (it makes excellent pappa al pomodoro; see page 169). And as my mom figured out at some point, you don't even have to peel the tomatoes before putting them into the food processor.

5 to 6 pounds ripe tomatoes, halved

1 onion, minced

¼ cup olive oil

1 teaspoon salt, or more to taste

3 tablespoons all-purpose flour

6 fresh parsley sprigs

6 fresh basil sprigs (or more parsley)

1 bay leaf

½ teaspoon dried thyme

¼ teaspoon fennel seeds

1 teaspoon coriander seeds, cracked

A 3-inch piece (about 1 teaspoon crumbled) dried orange peel

6 garlic cloves, crushed and peeled

Tomato paste if needed

Coarsely chop the tomatoes in a food processor (you may need to do this in batches).

Cook the onion in the olive oil in a large heavy pot over medium-low heat. Sprinkle in the salt and cook until the onion is tender and golden, about 10 minutes. Sprinkle in the flour and cook very gently for 3 minutes, until it begins to smell cooked; do not brown.

Meanwhile, wrap the parsley, basil, bay leaf, thyme, fennel, coriander, and orange peel in a square of cheesecloth and tie with kitchen twine.

Add the tomatoes, garlic cloves, and cheesecloth packet to the pot, cover, and cook over low heat for 10 minutes to bring out the liquid from the tomatoes. Uncover and simmer until thickened and sweet, 1 to 3 hours, depending on the type and ripeness of the tomatoes and the quantity; stir often to prevent scorching.

If the sauce seems thin, add tomato paste a few tablespoons at a time. Serve, or let cool, remove the cheesecloth bag, squeezing out any liquid, and freeze in heavy plastic bags or airtight containers.

Makes about 3 quarts (can be doubled or tripled)

PAPPA AL POMODORO

How to turn a container of tomato sauce and some stale bread into a quick dinner. This stewy soup is excellent after a large antipasto course, which at our house usually includes olives, salami, and a fennel salad (see page 75). If basil is not in season, add a few leaves of sage instead.

¼ cup extra-virgin olive oil

1 garlic clove, minced

¼ teaspoon red pepper flakes, or to taste

4 cups Julia Child's Tomato Sauce (page 167) or other best-quality tomato sauce

6 cups cubed stale or toasted bread, preferably from a crusty, hearty peasant loaf

¼ cup freshly grated Parmesan cheese, plus extra for garnish

⅓ cup fresh basil leaves, cut into ribbons

Olive oil or Toasted Chile Oil (page 126) for drizzling

Combine the extra-virgin olive oil, garlic, and pepper flakes in a medium pot and cook over low heat until the garlic is just turning gold. Stir in the tomato sauce and heat to a simmer. Stir in the bread, cheese, and ¼ cup of the basil and cook for a few minutes, using a potato masher to integrate the ingredients into a thick soup.

Serve in shallow bowls, garnished with the remaining basil, cheese, and a drizzle of olive or toasted chile oil.

Makes 4 servings

CORN FRITTERS

Pan-frying on a hot day is not anyone's idea of fun, but it must be done at least once a summer. Corn fritters are a secret weapon I love to pull out at the end of the season. Since they are never served in restaurants and rarely homemade, they are always greeted with surprise—joy, even.

3 ears corn, husks and silk removed

⅓ cup milk

1 large egg

1 teaspoon sugar

½ teaspoon baking powder

Coarse salt

¼ teaspoon freshly ground black pepper

¼ cup yellow cornmeal

¼ cup all-purpose flour

2 tablespoons vegetable oil

Maple syrup for serving

Preheat the oven to 200 degrees.

To remove the corn kernels, cut off the tip of each cob, stand it in a wide shallow bowl, and, with a sharp knife, slice downward to remove the kernels. Add the milk, egg, sugar, baking powder, ½ teaspoon salt, and the pepper to the bowl and mix well. Fold in the cornmeal and flour.

Line a rimmed baking sheet with paper towels. Heat 1 tablespoon of the oil in a large nonstick skillet over medium heat. Drop batter into the pan by heaping tablespoons and fry until golden brown, about 2 minutes per side. Transfer to the prepared baking sheet, sprinkle with salt, and put in the oven. Repeat with the remaining oil and batter. The fritters can be kept warm in the oven for up to 30 minutes.

Serve hot, with maple syrup for dipping.

Makes 4 to 6 servings

SKIRT STEAK WITH
SPICY CUCUMBER SALAD

As I remember it, I spent every summer of the 1990s fussing over flank steaks: marinating them in soy, studding them with garlic, devising red wine sauces—all to make them taste more like steak. Thank goodness I finally discovered skirt steak, a far juicer and tastier cut.

Now, I feel that being able to cook a steak and leave it alone is a sign of a well-adjusted adult cook. If steak is cooked well—and that means not fussing with it when it's on the grill or in the pan—it needs no embellishment. However, if you want to be the tiniest bit impressive, this spice mix lifts the flavors just enough.

A great chef in Cambridge, Massachusetts, Steve Johnson of Rendezvous, made this salad for me on a gorgeous August day in the galley kitchen of his houseboat, a tiny craft that looks just like a bath toy. It is great with jasmine rice next to steak or lamb, or grilled local bluefish, just how Steve served it on the deck of the Blue Sky.

FOR THE SALAD

¾ cup fresh lime juice (about 6 to
    12 limes)

¼ cup sugar

2 tablespoons salt, or to taste

1 tablespoon sambal oelek (or any
    hot sauce), to taste

1 tablespoon fish sauce

1 small red onion, thinly sliced

1½ pounds cucumbers, peeled,
    halved lengthwise, seeded, and
    sliced

1 tablespoon chopped fresh
    mint

1 tablespoon chopped fresh
    cilantro

FOR THE STEAK

1 teaspoon pink peppercorns

1 teaspoon black peppercorns

A dozen allspice berries

Large pinch of red pepper flakes

Skirt steak (2 to 3 pounds), cut   Salt
    into pieces that fit on your grill
    if necessary

To make the dressing: At least 2 hours before serving, combine the lime juice, sugar, salt, sambal, and fish sauce in a small bowl. Add the red onion and mix well. Refrigerate for at least 2 hours, or as long as overnight.

To make the steak: Heat a charcoal grill or heavy skillet until very hot.

Pound or grind the peppercorns, allspice, and pepper flakes together until coarsely ground. Rub this all over the steaks.

When ready to cook, sprinkle the steaks all over with salt. Grill, turning once, until crusty outside but still rare in the middle, about 5 minutes per side. Transfer to a platter and let rest for 5 minutes.

Meanwhile, assemble the salad. Lift the onions out of the dressing and combine them with the cucumber, mint, and cilantro in medium bowl. Spoon in a few tablespoons of dressing, mix, and season to taste with more dressing, salt, or sambal. (Reserve the remaining dressing.)

Cut the steak into serving pieces and divide among plates. Using a slotted spoon, arrange the salad on the plates. Trickle a little extra dressing over each serving.

Makes about 6 servings (can be doubled)

CRISSCROSS ZUCCHINI
WITH BASIL MAYONNAISE

What to do with zucchini in August? Grilled halves get boring; coins are harder to cook. Try this fresh-faced approach, adapted from a recipe from vegetable genius Deborah Madison.

FOR THE MAYONNAISE

About 4 fresh basil sprigs

½ cup mayonnaise (homemade if you are so inclined)

Fresh lemon juice to taste (¼ to ½ lemon)

Salt and freshly ground black pepper

About 20 small to medium zucchini

Olive oil

Salt and freshly ground black pepper

Lemon wedges

To make the mayonnaise: Bring a few cups of water to a boil in a small pot. Swish the basil sprigs around in it for 30 seconds, then run them under cold tap water. Dry on paper towels, then cut the leaves into thin ribbons or finely chop.

Mix the basil with the mayonnaise in a small bowl. Squeeze in the juice of ¼ lemon, and taste. Add more lemon if needed, and salt and pepper to taste. Transfer to a serving bowl.

Cut the zucchini lengthwise in half. Using the tip of a small knife, deeply score the cut surfaces in a crisscross pattern, without cutting through the skin. Brush the cut surfaces with olive oil and sprinkle with salt and pepper.

Heat a large cast-iron or heavy nonstick skillet and film the bottom with olive oil. Set the zucchini, cut side down, in a single layer in the pan and cook until golden, about 8 to 10 minutes. (You may have to do this in batches.) Turn the halves over, add a little water to the skillet to create steam, and cook on the second side just until tender when pierced with a knife. Arrange on a platter and serve hot or at room temperature, garnished with lemon wedges. Top each zucchini half with a small blob of mayonnaise.

Makes 8 to 10 servings

LEMON–BROWN BUTTER SHORTBREAD

Thank goodness pastry chefs never get tired of experimenting with shortbread. The classic version is great, but mine is to plain shortbread as the iPhone is to the Blackberry: superior in every aspect, including engineering, fun, and function. Note that it's best to begin this shortbread the day before you plan to serve it for the best texture. It is spectacular with summer fruits of all kinds.

12 tablespoons (1½ sticks)
  unsalted butter
½ cup lightly packed dark brown
  sugar
1 teaspoon vanilla extract

2 teaspoons grated lemon zest
½ teaspoon sea salt
1½ cups all-purpose flour
Granulated, Demerara, or
  turbinado sugar for sprinkling

Lightly grease a 9½-inch fluted tart pan with a removable bottom. Or, if you don't have a tart pan, line an 8-inch square cake pan with foil, leaving an overhang on two opposite sides so you can lift the shortbread out of the pan.

Melt the butter in a small saucepan over medium-low heat, then cook until the milk solids sink to the bottom, turn golden brown, and smell toasty; be careful not to burn the butter. Remove from the heat.

Combine the brown butter with the brown sugar, vanilla, zest, and salt in a medium bowl. Add the flour and mix until incorporated. Spread the dough evenly in the prepared pan. Let stand for at least 2 hours, or, preferably, overnight. (Do not refrigerate.)

Preheat the oven to 300 degrees.

Bake the shortbread for 45 minutes. Remove the pan from the oven, but leave the oven on. Lightly sprinkle the surface of the shortbread with sugar. Let cool for 10 minutes.

Very carefully remove the sides of the tart pan. Or, carefully remove the shortbread from the pan using the foil as a sling. Use a very sharp thin knife to cut it into 12 wedges or 9 squares. Carefully place the slices slightly apart on a baking sheet lined with parchment and return them to the oven for 15 minutes to toast lightly. Cool on a wire rack.

Makes 12 wedges or 9 squares

THE FARMERS' MARKET CHALLENGE

by KIM SEVERSON

There are so many ways Julia thinks she has the upper hand when we cook together in New York City. She usually does. She grew up there, and she knows places to go that might take me another ten years to discover. She has tricks and skills and the power of history behind her.

Perhaps the biggest advantage is a seasonal one. She knows when to buy strawberries and who sells the best radishes.

This made our fight at the farmers' market particularly challenging.

I have lived in a lot of places. I've had to learn to embrace a Midwest tomato season, a California tomato season, a Seattle tomato season, and even an Anchorage tomato season (although that really involved wandering around a glassed-in porch, ever hopeful that I could coax some fruitiness from the Arctic summer sun).

But Ms. Moskin, she's had the same region's season her whole life. She knows when the peaches will be at their best, and the rhythms of the corn and the tomatoes. In New York, that's really the big three. Those, and Concord grapes. And it was with the grapes that I planned to beat her.

The challenge: cook a meal from the overabundance that comes at the moment in the summer when you are just beginning to entertain the idea that soon you might not be able to look at another tomato or piece of corn. You aren't there yet, but it's coming.

Since summer is high grilling season, we added another layer of competition: flank versus skirt steak, with my love of a good Italian salsa verde over her belief that unadorned grilled meat—especially a flavorful skirt steak—is best. As I have mentioned before, for such a smart girl, she has some funny ideas.

Salsa verde, which you can really do with whatever herbs you have on hand as long as you stick to the caper, anchovy, and olive oil base, is a miracle. It's a great counterpoint to the lean flank steak, bringing out its beefiness but preventing the one-note-flavor problem that comes with eating plain meat.

My game plan was to scallop the tomatoes, a nice, warm break from the endless tomato salads of summer. The dish was inspired by my father's mom, a Midwest scalloper of the highest order, and the talented Ina Garten. I'd add some simple pickles to the table, made from carrots and young turnips. And then, my killer Concord grape pie.

I tasted one my first summer on the East Coast, during weekend on Cape Cod. I had never eaten Concord grapes except as they had been translated into the artificial tastes in soda pop or bubble gum. But that pie! It's what the jelly on my childhood sandwiches could only hope to be.

The thing about a grape pie is that it seems like a lot of work, skinning all those grapes. But the insides just pop out easy as, well, pie. Then the skins go back into the pot, simmering into a filling with a slightly meaty texture. The trick is to make it not too sweet.

Of course, Julia scoffed.

"No one likes warm grapes," she said.

But in truth, she had gone through a humiliating grape clafoutis experience with her family. And we were at her family's house upstate for this battle, so I think the wounds were especially fresh.

So who won? Well, she did pull out all the stops, frying such delicious corn fritters that people could talk of not much else. And while I'll give her the skirt steak, she was clearly wrong on the salsa verde point. Just ask her parents.

And ask them about the grape pie too. They sneaked into the kitchen the next day and finished it off when she wasn't looking.

GRILLED FLANK STEAK
WITH SALSA VERDE

Flank steak is very forgiving, and it cooks quickly. Even overcooking it past medium-rare won't hurt. The trick is to let it rest well, then cut it on the bias, against the grain. A charcoal grill always adds more flavor, but this preparation works well on a gas grill, which makes it an easy weeknight meal. Although flank steak takes well to marinades, a little garlic and some salt and pepper is all you need when you serve it with the salsa verde.

1½ pounds flank steak
2 garlic cloves, cut in half
Lots of salt and freshly ground
  black pepper

Italian Salsa Verde (recipe follows)

An hour before you plan to cook, put the flank steak on a cookie sheet and rub the cut sides of the garlic all over it. Sprinkle generously with salt and pepper. Let come to room temperature.

Prepare a hot charcoal grill or heat a gas grill to medium-high.

Add the steak to the grill and cook for about 4 minutes per side for medium-rare. Transfer to a platter and let rest for 10 minutes.

Slice the steak against the grain, angling the knife at about 45 degrees. Spoon about half the salsa verde over the top, then serve the rest at the table.

Makes 6 servings

Italian Salsa Verde

This is a miracle sauce that adds immediate interest to steak. It's also a great way to use up herbs. The parsley should be a constant, but you can substitute other herbs like chervil for these, or leave out the tarragon or basil if you forgot to pick it up at the store.

⅓ cup chopped fresh parsley
3 tablespoons *each* chopped
  chives, tarragon, and basil
1 shallot, minced
1 tablespoon capers
2 anchovy fillets

Grated zest of 1 lemon
2 tablespoons red wine vinegar
½ cup olive oil
Salt and freshly ground black
  pepper

Throw everything except the oil and salt and pepper into a blender or food processor and pulse a few times. Add the oil and pulse a couple more times. Taste and add a bit of salt and pepper. This can be made a day ahead and refrigerated, or left in a bowl on the counter if you are going to use it that day.

Makes 2 cups

PICKLED VEGETABLES

This recipe comes from my friend Robin Davis, who edits the food section for the *Columbus Dispatch* and who taught me much about cooking when we worked together at the *San Francisco Chronicle*. You can use daikon radish or turnips for this recipe, too.

1 pound thin young carrots, turnips, radishes, and/or cauliflower flowers, in any combination.

3 jalapeños, halved lengthwise and seeded

¼ cup minced fresh dill

2 teaspoons kosher salt

Scant ½ teaspoon crushed black peppercorns

1¼ cups white wine vinegar

1¼ cups water

¼ cup sugar

Prepare the vegetables by cleaning, removing tips and tails if appropriate, and making sure all of them are about the same thickness—cut some in half if need be.

Fill a medium bowl with ice and water. Blanch the vegetables in a pot of boiling water for 2 minutes. Drain and immediately transfer to the bowl of ice water to cool. Drain well.

Pack the vegetables and jalapeños into a 1-quart jar.

Combine the dill, salt, pepper, vinegar, water, and sugar in a saucepan and bring to a boil. Pour over the vegetables (you may have extra liquid). Cap the jar and let cool to room temperature, then refrigerate for at least 2 days. The vegetables will keep for 2 months.

Makes 1 quart

SCALLOPED TOMATOES

Versions of this dish abound. When I moved south to Atlanta, I found them in both fancy restaurants and roadside country diners. The version I still love the best, though, comes from Long Island. This is delicious hot from the oven, but at room temperature, it makes a great neighbor to eggs the next morning.

2½ pounds ripe tomatoes (smaller, less juicy ones work best), cut into large dice
3 garlic cloves, minced
2 tablespoons sugar
2 teaspoons salt
6 tablespoons olive oil
2 generous cups bread cubes from a white country loaf

½ cup julienned fresh basil leaves
1 teaspoon freshly ground black pepper
⅛ teaspoon cayenne pepper
1 cup freshly grated Parmesan cheese

Preheat the oven to 350 degrees.

Combine the tomatoes, garlic, sugar, and salt in a bowl. Set aside.

Heat 4 tablespoons of the olive oil in a large sauté pan over medium-high heat. When it starts to shimmer, add the bread cubes, stir, and toast, stirring frequently to make sure they cook evenly, until they start to get browned, about 5 minutes. Turn the heat down to medium, add the tomatoes, and cook, stirring frequently, for about 5 more minutes. Turn off the heat and stir in the basil and peppers.

Spread the mixture in a shallow baking dish and sprinkle with the cheese. Drizzle with the remaining olive oil and bake for 40 minutes, or until the top browns nicely and the tomatoes are bubbling.

Makes 6 to 8 servings

CONCORD GRAPE PIE

This pie requires Concord grapes, which makes it a very seasonal and regional pie. Some people swear by instant tapioca to thicken it, but I find flour works just as well and gives it a little silkier texture. If the filling seems too runny, give it time to cool and set up. The pie may bubble over as it bakes, so put a baking sheet on the rack below the rack holding the pie to catch any drips.

FOR THE CRUST
2½ cups all-purpose flour
1 teaspoon salt
½ pound (2 sticks) plus
  2 tablespoons very cold unsalted
  butter, cut into small pieces

Ice water

FOR THE FILLING
5 cups Concord grapes
¾ cup sugar (a little more if the
  grapes are particularly tart)
¼ cup all-purpose flour

1 tablespoon fresh lemon juice
1 tablespoon cold unsalted
  butter, cut into pieces

To make the crust: Put the flour and salt in a bowl and whisk to combine. With a pastry cutter or your thumbs and index fingers, break the butter into the flour mixture, leaving some pea-sized pieces and some finer pieces. Sprinkle with a few tablespoons of ice water, mixing gently until the dough holds together; you may add a little more water.

Pull the dough into a ball, turn it out onto a floured surface, and form into 2 disks. Wrap in plastic wrap and refrigerate for at least a couple of hours, or overnight.

Position the racks in the middle and lower third of the oven and preheat the oven to 375 degrees.

When ready to make the pie, on a lightly floured surface, gently roll one piece of dough into an 11-inch circle, working from the inside out. Drape it in a 9-inch pie tin and trim.

To make the filling: Squeeze the grapes and pop out the pulp inside. Put the pulp in a saucepan and the skins in a bowl. Add the sugar, flour, and lemon juice to the skins and mix well.

Bring the pulp just to a boil and boil gently, stirring frequently, until the seeds separate out, about 6 minutes. Place a strainer over the bowl of skins and pour in the pulp, using a wooden spoon to force the pulp through the sieve. Mix well.

Roll out the second piece of dough to an 11-inch circle.

Pour the filling into the pastry-lined pie tin. Top with the pieces of chilled butter. Cover with the second sheet of dough, trim if needed, and press the edges together. Make a few slits in the top.

To make a lattice top: Use a sharp knife and cut the dough round into 8 long strips and arrange across the top of the pie.

Put a baking sheet on the bottom oven rack to catch drips and put the pie on the rack above it. Bake for about 50 minutes, or until the top is golden and the filling is bubbling. Let cool until warm.

Makes one 9-inch pie

SEPTEMBER

THE WEEKDAY CHALLENGE

THE WEEKDAY CHALLENGE

by KIM SEVERSON

The real test of any cook comes on Tuesday night. Work was hard and there's still more to do after dinner. Homework needs to be checked and laundry needs to be folded. There may be baseball practice or a community meeting. A spouse is likely behaving in a manner that is not at all helpful. And, of course, people are hungry.

Most of us don't have the access to takeout that Moskin does. She can get pretty much anything delivered to her apartment door on the Upper West Side in a blink. (Oh, and have I mentioned that she has help? Lots of help? Parents just around the corner. A beloved nanny. Don't make me continue.)

Moskin also has the kind of refrigerator I used to when I spent most of my time testing recipes and writing about food. It's filled with all kinds of wonderful odd little bits of this and that, exotic sauces and special cheeses and perfect, unusual vegetables you're not going to pick up at the Piggly Wiggly.

Anyone can make a meal with a fridge like that! But now that I write more about breaking news than beautiful food, I have become like most of America. That is, I live in a city without decent delivery food and only limited access to specialty food shops. There are no perfect roast chickens, local vegetables, or warm baguettes to be had as I stroll home from work.

I drive to the grocery store, carefully schedule trips to the infrequent farmers' markets near me, and rely, mostly, on a well-stocked pantry of staples.

As a result, Tuesday supper depends largely on my wit and a budget. But, I tell you, it can be done. Delicious food can be on your table in less than an hour.

The key is learning to manage your kitchen. A well-managed kitchen is a thing of beauty. It means you always have a box of pasta, some chicken stock, and a few vegetables around.

Or perhaps there is a bit of cold steak and some leftover green beans to work into a steak salad. A dozen eggs, some toast, and some zucchini can become a peasant Italian dish, as it was in my house growing up.

And if you plan ahead a little, there will be plenty in that fridge to create a pasta dish, which could not be easier, and which provides not only dinner but also lunch for the kids the next day.

Now, Moskin has her methods for pasta. I know. It is clever, and it is delicious. Fine. I offer here two simpler pastas, one very kid-friendly and one sophisticated enough for a guest but easy enough for a weeknight.

And don't dismiss your ability to produce a roasted chicken on a school night. Try to set it up the day before, or in the morning if you have a minute or two. That way, you can have someone turn on the oven to preheat before you get home, or even have someone put the chicken in the oven while you're stuck in traffic.

You won't regret that Moskin is sitting there in her Manhattan apartment, eating dan dan noodles and gelato and wondering how people in the suburbs do it night after night.

ROAST CHICKEN IN A POT

This is really the easiest thing to do for a big payoff on a busy weeknight. I learned it from Thomas Keller of The French Laundry and Per Se. But don't let that intimidate you. The guy likes simple, delicious food too, and I have streamlined the recipe. And feel free to use the vegetables you have on hand.

If you can bear it, prepare the whole thing the night before and put the pot in the fridge. Have the first person home in the afternoon take the pot out, then you can throw it in the oven as soon as you walk in the door. In an hour, you'll have dinner. Depending on the size of your family, you may also have lunches for the next day. And if you are really ambitious, you can boil the carcass for a little bit of stock for the freezer.

One 3- to 4-pound chicken (the best you can find)
Salt and freshly ground black pepper
1 tablespoon olive oil
3 russet (baking) potatoes or 5 new red potatoes, thickly sliced

2 carrots, peeled and thickly sliced
2 onions, quartered
2 celery stalks, cut into thick chunks
3 fresh thyme sprigs or ½ teaspoon dried thyme

| 1 bay leaf | 3 tablespoons unsalted butter, |
| 1 lemon, cut in half | cut into small pieces |

Preheat the oven to 375 degrees.

Remove any big pieces of fat from the chicken. Salt liberally inside and out and grind pepper all over the skin.

Add the olive oil to an ovenproof pot (Le Creuset is good) or large deep roasting pan and rub it around, then add the vegetables and herbs, tossing to distribute everything.

Stuff the lemon halves into the chicken cavity and set the chicken on top of the vegetables. Dot the skin with the butter and roast for about an hour (about 17 minutes per pound is a good guide); a leg will feel loose when the chicken is done. Remove the chicken to a cutting board and let it sit for about 10 minutes.

Meanwhile, remove the bay leaf and see if the vegetables need a bit more seasoning.

Cut the chicken into parts: Remove the legs first, then cut the thighs and drumsticks apart. Remove the wings, then the 2 breasts. Slice the breast meat from the bone and then slice crosswise into thick pieces.

Serve the vegetables in a bowl and the chicken on a platter.

Makes 6 servings, or 4 servings with leftovers

SAMMY'S PASTA

This is a dish I developed with my daughter, Samantha. Or, more accurately, I developed it because she wanted all the things that are in here on various nights, and it just made sense to put them together. The key is letting her put the pasta in the pot and add the "sprinkle cheese," as she calls grated Parmesan, at the end—it's all about the buy-in when you're trying to get kids to eat.

Starting the dish with raw chicken gives it a richer flavor, but you can easily use leftovers from a roast chicken or the meat from a grocery store roasted bird.

8 ounces ziti, rigatoni, or
  other short dried pasta
1 large shallot, sliced
3 tablespoons olive oil
12 ounces boneless, skinless
  chicken breasts, cut into
  bite-sized chunks, or about
  1½ cups shredded cooked
  chicken
1 teaspoon salt

Scant ½ teaspoon freshly ground
  black pepper
8 ounces broccoli florets, about
  1½ cups (you can sub other
  green vegetables, like green
  beans)
1 cup chicken broth, or as needed
1 lemon, cut in half
½ cup freshly grated Parmesan
  cheese

Bring a large pot of salted water to a boil and add the pasta.

Meanwhile, cook the shallot in the oil in a large sauté pan over medium heat until softened. Turn the heat to medium-high, add the raw chicken, salt, and pepper, and cook until the chicken is just done, about 5 minutes. Alternatively, warm the cooked chicken in the pan.

About 3 minutes before the pasta is done, add the broccoli to the pot and cook until the pasta and broccoli are just barely al dente. Drain and add to the chicken.

Toss the pasta with about half the chicken broth and simmer for a couple of minutes. Squeeze the juice of the lemon over all and stir. Add more chicken broth if it seems dry.

Serve immediately, passing the cheese.

Makes 6 servings, or 4 with leftovers

JANET'S PASTA

There are a lot of versions of this dish, and you can use a few different kinds of short pasta such as fusilli or gemelli. I learned this version from Bay Area cook Janet Fletcher when I was working at the *San Francisco Chronicle*. With a well-staffed test kitchen and cooks like Janet around, I learned much about how to make food taste good.

This is an easy and forgiving recipe. Just remember to save some of the pasta water to help keep it saucy at the end.

1½ to 2 pounds broccoli rabe
1 pound orecchiette
⅓ cup extra-virgin olive oil
3 large garlic cloves, minced
Pinch of red pepper flakes
8 ounces hot Italian sausages,

preferably with fennel seed,
   removed from casings
Salt
Freshly grated Pecorino Romano
   cheese (Parmesan will do in a
   pinch)

Bring a large pot of salted water to a boil over high heat. Meanwhile, remove the tough stems from the broccoli rabe. Add the broccoli rabe to the boiling water and cook for about 3 minutes, to get the bitterness out. Transfer to a colander and run under cold water to stop the cooking. Drain well, then squeeze gently to remove excess water. Coarsely chop.

Throw the pasta into the boiling water and cook until al dente.

While the pasta is cooking, put the olive oil, garlic, and re pepper flakes in a large skillet. Add the sausage and cook over medium-low heat, breaking up the sausage with a fork, just until it loses most of its pinkness. Add the broccoli rabe and season with salt to taste, then stir to coat with the seasonings and gently heat through.

Set aside 1½ cups of the pasta water, drain the pasta, and return it to the warm pot over low heat. Add the sauce and toss well, moistening the pasta with some of the reserved water as needed.

Divide among warm bowls, sprinkle with cheese, and serve immediately. Pass more cheese at the table.

Makes 6 servings

EVERYONE'S CARROTS

I learned this trick from Pete Wells, my former editor at the *Times* Dining section. He wrote a lot about cooking with his son, Dexter. The syrup and butter make carrots even more appealing to kids. And since there are almost always carrots sitting in the vegetable drawer, it's a good way to add an easy side dish to a weeknight dinner. Everyone loves them.

2 pounds carrots, peeled and cut into coins
2 tablespoons maple syrup

2½ tablespoons butter
3 tablespoons water
Salt

Put everything, except salt, into a saucepan and cook over medium-high heat for about 5 minutes, stirring regularly. Turn the heat to medium-low, cover, and cook for another 5 minutes or until glazed and tender. Add a pinch of salt, stir, and taste to make sure the carrots are done.

Makes 6 servings

CUGOOCH

Almost everyone on the Zappa side of my family makes this dish of eggs and squash. It's cheap, easy, and satisfying. Because my mother and her siblings speak an Italian village dialect, no one knows the real Italian word for it. "I always imagined something like 'cugooch,'" says my scholarly brother, Kent. "The first 'c' is OK because it's before a 'u,' but the second consonant needs to be something different. Most Italian nouns end in a vowel, but it is dropped when the Zappas use this word. 'Cugucci' might work."

Whatever. It's a great way to use zucchini or, our preference, yellow squash. And although various branches of the family add pancetta or bacon, you can easily go meatless.

8 ounces bacon, chopped

1 medium onion, chopped

3 thin-skinned green Italian peppers, cored, seeded, and chopped

4 garlic cloves, minced

3 to 4 medium yellow squash or zucchini, chopped

1 bunch fresh basil, stemmed

1½ tablespoons fresh oregano or 1½ teaspoons dried oregano

Salt and freshly ground black pepper

4 large eggs

½ cup freshly grated Parmesan cheese

Cook the bacon in a large skillet until crisp. Remove from the pan. Add the onion and peppers to the pan and sauté gently over medium heat until just tender. This should take 3 or 4 minutes. Add the garlic, squash, bacon, herbs, and salt and pepper to taste and simmer until the mixture is stew-like, about 30 minutes.

Mix the eggs with a fork in a bowl and stir in the Parmesan cheese. Pour the egg mixture over the vegetables, turn off the heat, cover the pan, and let stand until the eggs are cooked, about 7 minutes.

Makes 6 servings

THE WEEKDAY CHALLENGE

by **JULIA MOSKIN**

Although Severson insists on painting me as the Carrie Bradshaw of the Dining section, my typical day is no different from that of most working parents. It begins far earlier than I would like, and by the time I get the kids out of the house, deal with the e-mails accumulated overnight, write a blog post, and get dressed for work, I am ready to go back to bed. (Doesn't everyone feel this way?) Instead, I have a full day ahead, at the end of which lies the dreaded question of what to have for dinner.

I understand why people assume that my children eat a healthy home-cooked dinner every night, and that my husband is the best-fed man in Manhattan. But the reality is much more peculiar.

Yes, sometimes I stay home and cook all day—usually something like White Asparagus Velouté with Seaweed Garnish or Malaysian Curried Noodle Soup. Yes, I take my husband out to eat—to just-opened Thai fusion gastropubs with no liquor license, or fabulous new pizzerias that don't take reservations, meaning that we have to wait an hour for a table and the cooks haven't yet figured out how to work the special oven imported from Naples.

Yes, my refrigerator is full of food: of watermelon rinds or maple vinegar or batches of kimchi at various stages of fermentation. There might be takeout from seven different northern Indian restaurants, or a full range of Sichuan jellyfish salads.

Somehow, very little of what I cook for work is actually edible. Like Alice in Wonderland heading off in one direction and finding herself going in the opposite, the more I eat for work, the less I cook at home.

I still have hope, but honesty compels me to admit that I don't yet have the hang of producing a delicious home-cooked dinner on weeknights. But since even my children are tired of the take-out options we have, I have learned a few work-arounds.

Cooking, it turns out, is not the hard part. Cooking is easy—thinking about cooking is hard. Cooking is easy—shopping and chopping are hard. So any short-cuts you can take (without ruining the taste of the food) are worth the extra

money. I buy precut carrot and celery sticks and chop them for soup. I lean on vegetables like snow peas and baby potatoes, which don't need peeling. And I try to think flexibly about what makes a "good" meal.

Pasta, after several swings of the pendulum, is a healthy dinner in my book (and this *is* my book, so I get to decide). Yes, I know the nutritionists say that refined flour is empty calories and essentially the same as Coca-Cola. I'm not buying it. The fact that everyone likes pasta; the fact that it can be loaded up with real ingredients like olive oil, Parmesan cheese, tomatoes, eggs, bacon, nuts, and greens; and the fact that it takes a while to eat, meaning that my children actually stay at the table and eat dinner with their parents, all outweigh the drawbacks of a simple starch. The kids I know are squeamish even about chicken legs and many of them have never seen a steak with a bone, but pasta is friendly. Pasta is a gateway for many flavors that children wouldn't try if presented separately: toss those pine nuts and lemon brown butter with the bowtie pasta, and they might surprise you.

I do have to come clean (i.e., secretly gloat) about one thing: my children eat salad. Lots and lots of salad, even bitter greens like endive, with avocados and tomatoes, all coated with a thick mustardy vinaigrette. I can't explain this phenomenon or pass it on, other than to say that I have put salad on the table almost every night since they were babies. At first, I didn't expect them to eat it at all; perhaps that's the trick. And salad-for-dinner—again, with our old friends bacon and eggs and toast to supplement it—is one of the fastest meals there is.

Toast is a fully respected side dish at our house, especially if the grill is already fired up, to give it a little smoky char. The kids like olive oil on their hot toast; the grown-ups get a rub of garlic (you don't even have to peel the clove, just cut it in half). If you stick the toast under a roast chicken, you don't have to make potatoes.

When my friend Lisa got married, her dear husband already had two medium-sized kids, and she knew that establishing her place in their family would be like getting through all the levels of Grand Theft Auto: slow and filled with pitfalls, with a sniper around every corner. She did it lovingly, and patiently, and using food as her weapon: taco night, chili-mac, and Refrigerator Chicken (a dish using all the condiments in the refrigerator door; see page 209). It worked. Families, like fan clubs and support groups, are built around shared passions. It doesn't matter so much if the passions are healthy; what matters is that they are shared.

THE MOSKIN METHOD FOR PASTA

OK, so Henry Ford perfected the assembly line, and Lego designers figured out how to build infinite systems from tiny pieces, many of which are under my son's bed. I claim this as the Moskin Method. It is a building-block system of dinner and cannot be contained in a straightforward recipe. It can, however, be served to everyone from visiting toddlers to vegan au pairs to your in-laws. Serving pasta with a choice of different toppings may seem obvious, but the effect is surprisingly delicious.

The method is adaptable, like those furniture systems that (provided you manage to keep track of the hardware, which I never do) allow you to turn a child's crib into a bed, and then into a desk, and finally into a pair of chic reading glasses. That is to say, it grows with your family. Before you know it, that butter-only toddler will be piling his pasta with bacon, chile flakes, cheese, and parsley.

FOR THE TOPPINGS

1 cup freshly grated Parmesan cheese, in a small serving bowl

About ⅓ cup chopped fresh parsley or cilantro, in a small serving bowl

Red pepper flakes, in a small serving bowl

A lemon

Unsalted butter

About ⅓ cup pine nuts

FOR THE OPTIONAL TOMATO-BACON SAUCE

8 ounces thick-cut bacon

3 to 4 cups homemade or best-quality jarred tomato sauce, such as Rao's

1½ to 2 pounds pasta

Put a large pot of salted water on to boil. Put the bowls of cheese, herbs, and pepper flakes on the table.

If making the tomato sauce: Put the bacon in a medium-heavy pot and turn the heat on low. Cook, turning occasionally, until the fat has rendered and the bacon is chewy-crisp, about 10 minutes. Lift out the bacon and pour off all but about 3 tablespoons fat from the pot.

Return the pot to the stove and add 3 cups tomato sauce. Stir and bring to a simmer. Crumble the bacon into large pieces and add half of them to the sauce. Put the remaining bacon in a small serving bowl and put it on the table. Cook the sauce until it tastes rich and tomato-y, adding more sauce if it cooks down too much. At serving time, put the hot tomato sauce on the table.

If not making the tomato sauce, zest the lemon, put the zest in a small serving bowl, and put on the table.

Cut the lemon in half.

When the water boils, add the pasta, stir well, and cover. When the water comes back to the boil, uncover, stir again, and cook until tender.

Meanwhile, put a chunk of butter in a small saucepan and melt it over medium-low heat. When it foams, throw in the pine nuts and cook, shaking the pan, until they turn brown and toasty. Squeeze the juice of the lemon into the pan, cupping your hand underneath to catch any pits. Simmer for a minute, then turn off the heat.

As soon as the pasta is tender, drain it, reserving a cup of the cooking water. Immediately return the pasta to the pot and toss in a chunk of butter. Add a splash of the cooking water, stir well, and cover until the moment of serving.

Pour half the hot pasta into a serving bowl for those who like plain pasta (or serve in the kitchen).

Pour the pine nuts and butter into the pasta remaining in the pot, add another splash of the cooking water, and toss to combine. Serve from the pot or in a serving bowl, passing the various toppings at the table.

Makes 4 to 6 servings

DINNER SALAD WITH MUSTARD-SHALLOT VINAIGRETTE, EGGS, AND GARLIC TOAST

You people just don't listen. I've been saying it for years: homemade vinaigrette lasts just as long in the fridge as that sweet, greasy stuff in bottles at the supermarket. Just make it once, keep it around, and see what happens. It might change your life.

This vinaigrette, my husband's culinary masterwork, actually gets better as it sits, because the shallots pickle in the vinegar, turning sweet and fiery. I will take the credit for teaching him the secret to any dressing: the vinegar/lemon juice/herbs/spices/mustard/etc. always have to be well combined BEFORE any oil goes in. Otherwise, the whole thing seizes up and can never be whisked smooth.

Bacon and eggs is no longer considered the perfect American breakfast, but I have reclaimed the combination as dinner and serve it often. Some people like their soft-yolked eggs tossed into the salad (as the French do), and some like them on the side. Same goes for the bacon, tomatoes, and pine nuts. So I put this meal together like a puzzle, with all the pieces spread out on the table. In the spring, there might also be some roasted asparagus; in August, corn on the cob. You get the idea.

FOR THE VINAIGRETTE
1 small shallot, finely chopped
White wine vinegar
Dijon mustard
Salt and freshly ground black
  pepper
Extra-virgin olive oil

FOR THE SALAD
Mixed greens, well washed and
  dried (2 large handfuls per
  person)

Avocado, peeled, pitted, and
sliced (½ per person)
Grape tomatoes, halved
Pine nuts, lightly toasted

Bacon, cooked and coarsely
crumbled
Poached or soft-boiled eggs

FOR THE TOAST

Crusty bread, white or whole-
grain, thickly sliced (or halved
lengthwise if using a baguette or
ciabatta)

Olive oil
1 large garlic clove, cut in half (no
need to peel)

To make the vinaigrette: Put the shallot in a medium jar with a tight-fitting lid. Pour in vinegar until it barely covers the shallot. Add a generous dollop of mustard, put on the lid, and shake well. Add about a teaspoon of salt and plenty of pepper and shake again. Pour in some oil and check the sides of the jar when the mixture settles: the goal is to have 1 part vinegar/mustard mixture to 4 parts oil. More oil is fine, up to a 1 to 6 ratio, depending on your taste. Shake and taste for salt and pepper and adjust accordingly.

Assemble the salad ingredients, placing the greens in a large bowl and the other ingredients in individual bowls.

To make the toast: Grill or toast the cut sides of the bread until well browned. Drizzle each slice (or the split loaves) lightly with olive oil. Rub the cut sides of the garlic lightly over the toast; the rough crumb of the bread will pick up the oil from the garlic. A few rubs on each slice are enough.

To serve, toss the greens well with enough dressing to lightly coat them. Serve in wide bowls, passing the warm toast and remaining ingredients at the table.

SPAGHETTI PIE

I have an unrequited crush on tortillas—not the round flatbreads, but the firm potato-and-egg dish served in wedges everywhere in Spain. I love it, but it does not love me back: I have never figured out how to cook the potatoes to the right doneness before adding the eggs. But leftover pasta, always in good supply in my refrigerator, works very well in a pie like this.

If you leave out the nutmeg, this will taste more like kid food. It reminds me of the old days, when cooking for vegetarians was simple: the *Moosewood Cookbook* was the only game in town, and every vegetable in it was cooked with lashings of butter, cream, and cheese.

3 tablespoons butter
1 onion, finely chopped
Salt
1 small garlic clove, minced
One 10-ounce package frozen leaf
    spinach, thawed and squeezed
    dry in a kitchen towel
¾ cup heavy cream
⅛ teaspoon freshly grated nutmeg
    (optional)
Freshly ground black pepper
About 6 cups cooked spaghetti
    or small-gauge short pasta
    (not ziti or rigatoni), at room
    temperature

8 large eggs, well beaten
1 cup grated cheese, such as
    mozzarella, Parmesan, or
    cheddar, or a combination
    (optional)
Tomato-Bacon Sauce (page 203;
    optional), warmed

Preheat the broiler (to low if possible).

Melt the butter in a large nonstick or cast-iron skillet over medium-high heat. Add the chopped onion, sprinkle with salt, and cook, stirring, until softened, about 5 minutes (reduce the heat as needed to prevent browning). Add the garlic and stir to combine; then add the spinach and cream, bring to a simmer, and cook, stirring, until thickened. Add the nutmeg, if using, then add salt and pepper to taste.

Add the pasta to the skillet and mix well. Gently pour the eggs over the top and cook over low heat. As the eggs begin to cook, lift up the edges to let the uncooked egg mixture run into the bottom of the pan. Once most of the mixture has set, leave it alone.

When the top is set but still shiny, sprinkle with the cheese, if using, and slide under the broiler. Watch like a hawk. As soon as the top is gilded and puffy, remove it. Serve immediately, cut into wedges. Spoon the tomato sauce on top, if desired.

Makes 4 servings

REFRIGERATOR CHICKEN

In addition to pasta and salad, every cook needs a fallback, foolproof recipe for chicken breasts. I was a chicken breast snob for years, and a teriyaki snob to boot. But then my dear pal Lisa, who is not troubled by food shame and likes to keep a big bottle of Saucy Susan around the house, introduced me to Refrigerator Chicken. It uses chicken breasts and all the condiments in the fridge door—and, of course, is highly flexible. Children love it.

FOR THE MARINADE

2 tablespoons ketchup

2 tablespoons duck sauce, Saucy Susan, apricot jam, sweet Thai chile sauce, or honey

2 tablespoons vinaigrette (such as Mustard-Shallot, page 205) or mild Italian dressing (not balsamic or creamy)

1 heaping teaspoon Dijon mustard

3 to 4 tablespoons soy sauce, or to taste

1 teaspoon hoisin sauce (optional)

2 dashes Sriracha or other hot sauce

About 1 tablespoon rice wine, dry sherry, or vermouth

1 garlic clove, minced

Lemon juice (optional)

2 pounds boneless, skinless chicken breasts, thinly sliced

To make the marinade: Combine all the ingredients in a baking dish and mix. Taste and adjust for a good balance of salty, sweet, spicy, and acid. Overall, the sauce should be more brown than red. If the mixture is too salty or sweet, add a squeeze of lemon.

Scoop out a few tablespoons of the marinade and set aside. Add the chicken to the baking dish and turn to coat well. Marinate 30 minutes to 2 hours.

The marinated chicken can be baked at 375 degrees, cooked on top of the stove in a nonstick skillet or grill pan, or grilled. (However, grilling will dry the chicken out very quickly, so cook for just a few minutes on each side.) While cooking, lightly brush the chicken with the reserved marinade. The mixture contains a lot of sugar; so it will scorch if cooked over high heat; watch carefully.

Makes 4 servings

UN-BAKED APPLES WITH
BROWN SUGAR AND LEMON

An easy, reasonably healthy dessert that is like a tarte Tatin without the crust. I love the taste of baked apples, but they are rather depressing to look at and no one likes to deal with the skin: this technique solves both problems. And elegantly, as one might expect from the English writer Elizabeth David, from whom this is adapted. She was a proto-type for food-obsessed, footloose women of the modern age. Serve it with shortbread cookies and heavy cream, ice cream, or thick Greek yogurt.

Apples (1 or 2 per person)
Brown sugar
Lemon peel, cut into strips about
  3 inches long and ½-inch wide

1 cinnamon stick
Butter

Core, peel, and thickly slice the apples. Put the cores and peels into a saucepan and add 1 teaspoon brown sugar and 1 piece of lemon peel for each apple. Add the cinnamon stick, cover with water, and bring to a boil. Boil until syrupy, about 10 minutes.

Put the apple slices in a nonstick skillet and dot with cold butter. When the syrup is done, pour it through a strainer over the apple slices. Cook over low heat until the apples are tender, about 10 minutes.

OCTOBER

THE BAKE-OFF CHALLENGE

OCTOBER

THE BAKE-OFF CHALLENGE

by JULIA MOSKIN

After a recent reshuffle in the *New York Times* newsroom, the Dining section ended up under the authority of a former political editor who thought food was "fun." He immediately decided to stage a pumpkin-pie-baking contest among the staff. He would be the judge. The amateurs, such as the fashion critics and copy editors, thought this would be a hoot. As an experienced baker, I found it a terrifying prospect: you never quite know what will happen with a pie. Reader, I bowed out. And as you will notice, there is no pie in this chapter. The closest thing is a pear brown Betty: same flavors, less stress.

Severson embraces stress and pressure. She sets herself impossible challenges, then meets them—not effortlessly, of course. She brings all of her friends along with her for a hair-raising ride of overcommitments, last-minute notions, and impossible deadlines.

Which means, I guess, that she is not as much of a perfectionist as I am. She is not afraid to fail, an important quality in becoming an adventurous cook. I hate doing things I'm not already great at. When I was younger, I didn't like going to new restaurants because I hated not knowing where the bathroom was. That really bothered me, and it will tell you something about the kind of perfectionist nut

job I am always in danger of becoming. Unlike Severson, I'm not competitive with others, only with myself.

The most competitive baker I've ever encountered was a woman I'll call Cindy, who had invented the cookie swap—or, at least, that was her claim. She certainly was the first person who cared enough about them to write a book's worth of rules for holiday cookie swaps, including mandatory sweaters and a ban on chocolate chip cookies, which she considered inappropriate for reasons I still wonder about. Interviewing her was a lesson in how to take all the fun out of baking.

Baking isn't always fun. You have to follow the directions minutely. I have spent many white-knuckle-nights with cakes that wouldn't cool, custards that set too fast, and piecrusts that glued themselves to the counter. Baking is the high-stakes challenge of the home kitchen, and I like a quiet life. Thus, this is a gentle chapter for me.

Except for my peanut butter cookies, which have a cup of revenge stirred in. My career as a stay-at-home mother lasted all of four months and is remembered by all as one long nervous breakdown. It's not like I was powering through a high-octane Wall Street career before I became a mom; in fact, I was a freelance writer

and spent most days having unstructured time at home in my pajamas. But when the baby arrived, I didn't know what to do with him all day, or what to do with myself when I couldn't read and write and cook as I pleased.

It wasn't pretty.

One of my few solaces was the walk from our apartment in the West Village to a bakery in Chelsea, where the peanut butter cookies were (and are) nourishing in every way. They are salty and sweet, soft and sandy, rich and caramelized at the same time. I spent so much time there that I finally braved the strangeness of breast-feeding in public, a distinctly odd feeling until you've done it. When feeding my soul with that cookie and my baby with milk at the same time, I felt a little less dark about the future.

Many prescriptions later, when I had recovered my senses and made the leap from stringer to *New York Times* staff reporter, I confessed my feelings to the bakery's owner and asked for the recipe. It wasn't for publication—I was pregnant again and living uptown, too far to walk with a stroller, and I wanted to ensure a steady supply of peanut butter cookies for myself.

Not to sound grand, but as a reporter for the *Times* Dining section, when I ask someone for a recipe, I generally get it. Not from this chef, who felt it was important for him to protect his intellectual property.

I (obviously) sulked over this for years. Sulking didn't help.

What helped? Finding the recipe online, posted by a home cook who had taken a cooking class with the owner. She didn't even like the cookies, but she'd heard that other people had a thing for them. The recipe worked like a charm the first time out. I even improved on it. It may have taken years, but revenge was sweet—and chunky. (Note to Severson: Moskin Wins Again!)

BILL YOSSES' DRIED FRUIT
DROP SCONES

Every morning, a selection of truly disgusting scones appears in New York bakeries: too sweet, too tough, too crumbly, underbaked. Years ago I tasted one at Soho's Dean & DeLuca that made me ecstatic, and I tracked down the source. But, sadly, the chef soon moved on, and with him the lovely, buttery, golden scones that had spoiled me for all others.

Much later, I went to Washington to interview him: the charming and kindhearted Bill Yosses, who turned out to be the pastry chef for President George W. Bush and then Barack Obama. Nothing makes you feel like a Real Journalist more than arriving for interviews at the White House (What's that, Severson? You've never worked in the White House? Goodness, how sad). In my case, I was there to write a profile of the pastry chef, but as I crunched down the gravel driveway toward the press room, I felt like Bob Woodward.

Bill showed me around the pastry kitchen (it's the second-floor window all the way to the right on the facade). And we checked out the beehives, tiptoed around the edges of the carpet in the Gold Room, and generally giggled at finding ourselves, after all this time, in such grand surroundings.

1½ cups all-purpose flour
1½ teaspoons baking powder
¼ cup sugar, plus extra for
sprinkling
½ teaspoon salt
6 tablespoons cold unsalted
butter, cut into small chunks

¼ cup heavy cream, plus extra for
brushing
1 large egg
½ cup chopped dried apricots
½ cup chopped dried prunes or
whole dried cherries

Preheat the oven to 375 degrees.

Sift the dry ingredients together.

In the bowl of a stand mixer fitted with the paddle attachment, combine the butter, cream, and egg. Add the dried fruits and dry ingredients and mix on low just until the dough comes together; do not overmix.

Using an ice cream scoop or a large spoon, drop the dough onto an ungreased baking sheet. Brush with cream and sprinkle with sugar. Bake for 8 to 10 minutes, until golden. Let cool on cookie sheet.

Makes 10 to 12 scones

PEANUT BUTTER SANDIES

The City Bakery is one of my favorite places to eat in New York, a bustling all-day canteen that serves all kinds of New Yorkers and all kinds of food: sweet and savory, breakfast and lunch, blueberry muffins and banh mi. Everything is good and some things are great, like the pretzel croissants and the sandy-soft peanut butter cookies. The City Bakery reminds me of the New York subway system (in a good way), because it's democratic and efficient, and the people-watching opportunities are great. As far as I know, its only flaw is that the owner refused to give me this recipe when I asked for it. So I connived this from a third-hand bootleg copy, posted online by a home cook who once took a cooking class from him.

Note there is no leavening in the dough, and the cookies will not spread out or rise while baking.

½ pound (2 sticks) unsalted butter, at room temperature
2 cups granulated sugar
⅔ cup packed light brown sugar
1 teaspoon salt, plus extra for sprinkling

2¼ cups (18 ounces) peanut butter, creamy or chunky
2 large eggs
2¼ cups all-purpose flour

Preheat the oven to 350 degrees and position a rack in the center. Line two baking sheets with parchment paper.

In the bowl of a stand mixer fitted with the paddle attachment, cream the butter, sugars, and salt until light and fluffy, at least 3 minutes. Add the peanut butter and eggs and mix well. Add the flour and mix just until well combined.

Using a small cookie scoop or a spoon, scoop the dough (2 to 3 teaspoons per cookie) onto the prepared sheets, leaving a 1 inch space between them. Sprinkle lightly with salt.

Bake for 8 to 10 minutes, until golden. Slide the cookies, still on the paper, onto a rack and let cool. The cookies are very crumbly, especially when warm.

Makes 3 to 4 dozen cookies

BACON-FAT GINGERSNAPS

Amazingly, the *New York Times* fashion critic, Cathy Horyn, is also an accomplished cook and intrepid baker. The equivalent would be if I, a food writer, were also a sleek fashion plate with a deep bench of vintage and modern pieces. This is certainly not the case, so I find her extremely impressive. She claims that these cookies are a Swedish-American tradition in her hometown of Coshocton, Ohio, but I feel they are the cookie equivalent of Paris Fashion Week: a modern, edgy take on a classic. They are truly remarkable, with a robust and smoky undertone that sets them apart from other gingersnaps.

¾ cup bacon fat (from 1½ to 2 pounds bacon), at room temperature

1 cup sugar, plus ¼ cup for rolling

¼ cup molasses (not blackstrap) or cane syrup, such as Steen's or Lyle's

1 large egg

2 cups all-purpose flour

1½ teaspoons kosher salt

2 teaspoons baking soda

2 teaspoons ground ginger

½ teaspoon ground cloves

½ teaspoon ground cinnamon

Combine all the ingredients in a food processor, and pulse until a smooth, stiff dough forms. Wrap the dough in plastic and chill in the refrigerator for a few hours.

Preheat the oven to 350 degrees. Line two baking sheets with parchment paper.

Put the ¼ cup sugar in a shallow bowl. Breaking off 1-tablespoon lumps, roll the dough into balls, drop into the sugar, roll to coat, and place 2 inches apart on the baking sheets.

Bake for 10 to 12 minutes, until the cookies are dark brown. Let cool on the baking sheets for a few minutes, then transfer to a rack to cool completely.

Makes 3 to 4 dozen cookies

CRANBERRY RIGHT-SIDE-UP CAKE

This cake is an homage to my all-time-favorite food writer, Laurie Colwin. Colwin published her recipe in *More Home Cooking*, an essay collection that came out after she died—much too young—in 1992. As I always tell aspiring authors, her books should live permanently on the bedside table of anyone who wants to write about food, and her taste in recipes was timeless.

Colwin called this recipe Nantucket Cranberry Pie, although it is in truth a buttery cake that sets off any sweet, tangy fruit beautifully. She said that she was unable to track its source, but that was in a pre-Internet world. A brief encounter with Google brought me quickly to the source of the recipe: *Cold-Weather Cooking* by Sarah Leah Chase, a wonderful writer and cook who lives in Massachusetts.

One 12-ounce bag cranberries
½ cup packed light brown sugar
1 tablespoon grated orange zest
½ teaspoon ground nutmeg or allspice
¾ cup chopped walnuts
2 large eggs

8 tablespoons (1 stick) unsalted butter, melted
¾ cup granulated sugar
1 teaspoon vanilla extract
¼ cup sour cream
1 cup all-purpose flour

Preheat the oven to 325 degrees. Butter an 8- or 9-inch round cake pan and line the bottom with parchment.

Combine the cranberries, brown sugar, orange zest, nutmeg, and walnuts in a bowl then spread evenly over the bottom of the pan.

Whisk the eggs in a medium bowl. Mix in the remaining ingredients until smooth. Pour the batter evenly over the cranberries.

Bake for about 1 hour, until the cake is just firm and browned on top. Let cool at least 20 minutes. Then, turn out onto a cake plate so that the fruit is on top. Peel off the paper. Serve warm or at room temperature, with whipped cream, heavy cream, or ice cream.

Makes one 8- or 9-inch cake

GOLDEN PEAR BROWN BETTY

I try to like the complicated desserts at the fancy restaurants I go to for work, but mostly it's a losing battle. After a big dinner, I want the basics: butter, sugar, fruit, and flour. This includes cakes, pies, crisps, crumbles, buckles, and compotes, as well as brown Betties, which use one of my all-time favorite ingredients: buttery bread crumbs. This is a free-form Betty; the pears and topping aren't baked together. Apart from the occasional mint-chocolate-chip milk shake or chocolate truffle, that's all I need from the sweet world. Most restaurant chefs seem to feel the same way: you almost never catch them eating dessert.

⅓ cup plus ¼ cup packed light
  brown sugar, or more to taste
3 pounds ripe pears, peeled,
  cored, and coarsely chopped
½ cup golden raisins or dried
  cherries
Fresh lemon juice
8 ounces stale bread, croissants,
  scones, or any other not-too-
  sweet baked item

3 tablespoons unsalted butter
1 teaspoon ground cinnamon
1 teaspoon ground allspice,
  nutmeg, or cloves, or a
  combination
Heavy cream, crème fraîche, or
  whipped cream for serving

Combine the ⅓ cup brown sugar, pears, raisins, and a splash of water in a large saucepan and bring to a simmer over low heat. Cover and simmer, stirring occasionally, until soft and chunky, 10 to 15 minutes. The mixture should be both tart and sweet: taste and adjust the flavor with sugar and lemon juice as necessary.

Pulse the bread into a coarse mix of crumbs and shards in a food processor.

Melt the butter in a large skillet over medium-high heat. Add the bread crumbs and cook, stirring, until they become crisp and golden. Turn off the heat and stir in the remaining ¼ cup sugar and the spices. Taste for sweetness, and sprinkle in more sugar if needed.

Serve the pear mixture warm, topped with a generous sprinkling of crumbs and a plop of cream.

Makes 6 to 8 servings

OCTOBER

THE BAKE-OFF CHALLENGE

by KIM SEVERSON

Usually, Ms. Moskin fights fair. At least mostly fair. Sure, she occasionally calls in a ringer to help her plan a menu, or gets a little extra help when we cook together. (I won't mention the times she set up separate child care while I had to cook with a three-year-old attached to my leg.) But generally, she wouldn't lie or cheat to try to win these challenges. At least, that's the premise I was operating under. Then, boom, she laid this one down: the bacon-fat gingersnap.

In my book, that's not fighting fair. First of all, she knows I am not a great baker. I do bake, yes. And I have been spending the past couple of years, while I have resided in the Deep South, perfecting my layer cakes and my biscuits. I try.

But, like many of you, I have limited patience in the kitchen. I like the thrill of a fast sauté and the hands-on nature of rolling meatballs or chopping vegetables. When I engage in cooking that takes patience—say, a long braise or a ragù—the fact that I can nudge the time and a few ingredients here and there, adjusting as I go, gives me comfort and confidence.

Not so with baking. You have to trust the chemistry, give in to the alchemy. You have to be exact, worrying over the height of the oven racks and the temperature of your eggs and the age of your baking powder.

So, baking isn't the strongest suit in my kitchen hand. Moskin knows this. That's why, when we were putting together our bake-off lists, she pulled out the one recipe I could never beat. Her gingersnaps, made soft and slightly savory with that devil, bacon fat, are cookies that have it all—surprise, deliciousness, and a beautiful old-fashioned piece of kitchen economy.

I lamented to friends, but they told me not to worry.

"Well, that leaves out the Jews, the Muslims, much of the Indian subcontinent, and the vegetarian crowd, so I'd bet on limited popularity for those cookies," said Cindy Burke, a great cook and my oldest and dearest friend.

"There are plenty of great gingersnap recipes," said Robin Davis, one of the women who taught me to cook. She runs a massive Christmas cookie contest every year at the *Columbus Dispatch*, where she is the food editor. Midwesterners know from cookies. And they are helpful. Robin sent some recipes for me to test, and I found a wonderful counterpoint to Moskin's gingersnap. It uses bits of toffee, not animal fat, as its secret ingredient.

To round out my baking battle, I turned to another great Midwesterner, my

mother. Every year at Thanksgiving she would bake date-nut bread in coffee cans and send it to all of her children, who were spread out all over the country. There are few things as good as a slice of her sweet bread topped with a thick smear of salted butter.

I adjusted to living in the South by making biscuits from all manner of sources. There was a recipe from Scott Peacock, who learned biscuits from the late, great Edna Lewis, champion of Southern cooking. There were biscuits from old Southern community cookbooks, and biscuits from Nathalie Dupree.

But the recipe I love best employs a technique I learned from baking guru Shirley Corriher. They're very wet to start, and so you get the added joy of tossing an ice cream scoop of the loose dough into a pan of flour. No rolling, no cutting. Just biscuits as light as an angel.

I played with several cakes but eventually landed on one that came to me when I was desperately depressed and pondering the meaning of life. I was attracted to it because I like white cake, fluffy frosting, and coconut cream pie. The cake gave it all to me, in loads. And it came from a soul sister who was going through the same thing I was. She made it for her daughter's birthday, so it has some extra love in it. SK, thanks for the cuatro leches cake. It saved me.

Last, a surprise I knew Moskin wouldn't think of. It's a steamed pudding that comes with a whole lemon inside. I learned about the famous Sussex Pond pudding when I was going deep on soft, steamed, cakey British puddings when I was writing about food for the *San Francisco Chronicle*. Marlena Spieler, a woman who has a recipe for everything (and, often, a cheese she has smuggled over from Britain in her bra), helped me figure this one out.

So there. I might not have a bacon-fat cookie, but I do have a roster of baked goods from women I love. And to me, that's winning.

ANNE SEVERSON'S COFFEE CAN DATE-NUT BREAD

Once I finally escaped to college, my mother kept me close by sending a package every Thanksgiving. The highlight was the coffee can in which she had baked date-nut bread. It was genius. She saved her Maxwell House cans all year, just so her kids and distant friends could get fresh loaves of sweet bread in a shippable container.

My brother Kent recently copied my mother's recipe exactly for me. He is an art conservator, so documentation is very important to him. Here are his "field notes" on my mother's handwritten recipe:

> *Taken from a 3 x 5" card in the file, decorated with flowers and vegetables, with the traditional "Recipe for" and "Serves," with "From the kitchen of . . ." below and lined for text. Typed on a manual typewriter.*

It was a bare-bones recipe, as most used to be when people knew how to cook. I've fleshed it out here.

1 cup chopped dates	1 cup sugar
2 cups boiling water	2 large eggs, beaten
2 teaspoons baking soda	2 tablespoons butter, melted

1 teaspoon vanilla extract

4 cups all-purpose flour

1 teaspoon salt

¾ cup pecans or walnuts, toasted
and roughly chopped

Preheat the oven to 350 degrees. Butter and flour four clean 12-ounce coffee cans.

Mix the dates, boiling water, and baking soda in a bowl. Set aside to cool slightly.

Mix together the sugar and eggs in a large bowl, then add the butter and vanilla and beat well. Sift the flour and salt together and add to the mixture, stirring just to combine. Gently mix in the dates and nuts, with their liquid, until just combined.

Distribute the batter among the cans, filling them about halfway. Bake for about 1 hour, or until a skewer inserted in the center comes out clean. Let cool on a rack.

Remove from the cans, wrap in plastic wrap, and mail to friends.

Makes 4 round loaves

CUATRO LECHES CAKE

Sara Kate Gillingham-Ryan, who runs theKitchn blog, gifted this cake to me. It takes a lot of time, and you have to use fresh coconut (though you could cheat, I suppose). Still, it's worth it. Good baking always is.

FOR THE CAKE

1½ cups cake flour

1½ teaspoons baking powder

½ teaspoon salt

8 tablespoons (1 stick) unsalted
   butter, at room temperature

1 cup sugar

4 large eggs, separated

⅓ cup evaporated milk

1 teaspoon vanilla extract

FOR THE LECHE GLAZE

1 cup coconut milk

½ cup sweetened condensed milk

¼ cup evaporated milk

¼ cup heavy cream

1 teaspoon vanilla extract

FOR THE TOPPING

2 cups heavy cream

⅓ cup confectioners' sugar

1 teaspoon vanilla extract

1 coconut, cracked open, flesh
   removed and shredded (about 1
   cup)

To make the cake: Preheat the oven to 350 degrees. Grease and flour a 9-inch round cake pan and line with a circle of parchment paper.

Whisk together the cake flour, baking powder, and salt in a medium bowl. Set aside.

Using a stand mixer, a handheld mixer, or a wooden spoon, cream the butter and ¾ cup of the sugar in a large bowl. Beat in the egg yolks until the mixture is uniform in texture and pale yellow. Stir in the evaporated milk and vanilla until well combined.

Beat the egg whites to soft peaks in a large bowl (if using a stand mixer and you don't have a second bowl, transfer the egg mixture to another large bowl and clean and dry the mixer bowl). Gradually add the remaining ¼ cup sugar and beat until the whites are glossy and stiff.

Fold one-third of the egg white mixture into the egg yolk mixture, then fold in one-third of the dry mixture. Alternate in this manner until all the ingredients are combined.

Transfer the mixture to the prepared baking pan. Bake for 35 to 45 minutes, until the top is golden brown and the cake springs back when touched lightly in the middle. Let cool for 10 minutes on a rack, then remove the cake from the pan, peel off the parchment, and allow to cool completely on the rack.

To make the leche glaze: Combine all the ingredients in a saucepan and heat over medium heat, stirring constantly, until bubbling. Remove from the heat and allow to cool slightly. It should be warm.

Slice cooled cake horizontally into 2 even layers. Place each layer on a large

I have found no better explanation on how to open a coconut than from Marion Cunningham in the *Fannie Farmer Cookbook:* "The easiest way to open a fresh coconut is to fling it onto a cement or a rock surface (not the kitchen floor). This is the way the monkeys do it, and they are the professionals."

Of course, a hammer and a chisel works well, too.

With either method, you will lose the liquid inside. Not to worry. This recipe calls for the meat only. Still, the liquid inside is good to drink. To capture it, place a large metal bowl over a damp towel, place the coconut in the bowl and then tap, catching the milk in the bowl.

Alternately, you can pierce the eyes of the coconut, drain the liquid, and bake it in a 400-degree oven for 10 or 15 minutes, then crack it with a hammer. The flesh can be pried from the shell a bit easier with this method. Peel off any brown membrane and grate on a box grater.

plate and spoon the glaze evenly over the layers, ¼ cup at a time, waiting about 5 minutes between pours to allow the cake to absorb the glaze. Cover and refrigerate for at least 4 hours, or preferably, overnight.

To make the topping: Beat the cream, sugar, and vanilla extract in a medium bowl until stiff peaks form.

To assemble the cake: Place 3 strips of parchment in a triangle on a cake platter: the triangle should be large enough so the cake can rest on top without any of the plate showing between the cake and the parchment. Carefully peel each cake layer off its plate. Place the original bottom layer cut side up on the platter. Using an offset spatula or a wide knife, spread a thin layer of the topping over the layer. Then dump about a cup of topping in the middle and spread evenly over the layer, right up to the sides. Carefully place the second layer cut side down on top. Top the cake with the remaining topping, and spread the cream over the top and down the sides.

Decorate the top and/or sides of the cake with the coconut, pressing it carefully into the cream. Carefully pull away the parchment strips, leaving a clean plate.

Makes one 9-inch layer cake

Note: Cake layers can be made a day ahead, wrapped in plastic, and stored at room temperature.

ANGEL BISCUITS

I have had biscuit lessons from many people. I learned to be sure to use fresh baking powder, to be as gentle as a baby's bath when kneading the dough, and not to twist the cutter when making the circles. Then I watched Shirley Corriher make these biscuits, and I realized they are exactly the kind of biscuit I want to eat—airy and crunchy on top—and foolproof for an amateur baker like me.

2½ cups self-rising flour (if self-rising flour is not available, combine 1 cup all-purpose flour, 1 teaspoon salt, and 1½ teaspoons baking powder)
1 tablespoon sugar
½ teaspoon salt

⅛ teaspoon baking soda
3 tablespoons vegetable shortening
¾ cup plus 2 tablespoons buttermilk
2 tablespoons unsalted butter, melted

Position a rack just above the center of the oven and preheat the oven to 450 degrees. Spray an 8-inch round cake pan with nonstick spray.

Combine 1½ cups of the flour, sugar, salt, and baking soda in a bowl. With your fingers or a pastry cutter, work the shortening into the flour mixture until there are no shortening lumps larger than a small pea. Stir in the buttermilk and let the dough stand for 2 to 3 minutes. It will be very wet.

Pour the remaining cup of flour onto a plate or into a pie pan. Flour your hands well. Using a large spoon or a small ice cream scoop, scoop a biscuit-sized lump of wet dough (a little larger than a golf ball) into the flour.

Sprinkle some of the flour on top and shape the dough into a soft round, gently shaking off any excess flour, then put it in the cake pan. The dough is so soft that it will not hold its shape; as you continue shaping the biscuits, push them tightly against each other in the cake pan so that they will rise up rather than spread out.

Brush the biscuits with the melted butter and put in the oven. Increase the oven temperature to 475 degrees and bake for 15 to 18 minutes, until the biscuits are lightly browned. Cool for a minute or two in the pan, and serve warm.

Makes about 12 biscuits

GINGER SPICE "BEAT MOSKIN" TOFFEE-KISSED COOKIES

This recipe came from Robin Davis of Columbus, Ohio, who got it from Teri Ralston of New Albany, Ohio, and Loretta Berrigan from Circleville, Ohio. Good cookie recipes love to be passed down.

2 cups all-purpose flour
2 teaspoons ground ginger
2 teaspoons baking soda
1½ teaspoons ground cinnamon
1 teaspoon ground allspice
⅛ teaspoon ground cloves
¾ teaspoon salt
12 tablespoons (1½ sticks) unsalted butter, at room temperature

1 cup packed dark brown sugar
1 large egg
3 tablespoons unsulfured molasses
1 cup toffee bits, such as Bits 'o Brickle
½ cup turbinado sugar

Whisk the flour, ginger, baking soda, cinnamon, allspice, cloves, and salt in a medium bowl.

Using a handheld mixer, beat the butter and brown sugar in a large bowl on medium speed until blended. Beat in the egg and molasses, beating just until blended. Stir in the flour mixture, then the toffee bits. Cover and refrigerate for 1 hour.

Preheat the oven to 350 degrees. Line two baking sheets with parchment.

Use a 1½-inch cookie dough scoop or large tablespoon to scoop mounds of dough, then roll into balls and roll in the turbinado sugar, pressing gently so it adheres. Arrange the balls 2 inches apart on the prepared sheets. Bake for 13 to 15 minutes, or until the tops have cracked but the cookies are still soft in the middle. Cool on the sheets for 5 minutes, then transfer to racks to cool completely.

Makes about 32 cookies

STEAMED MEYER LEMON PUDDING

Traditional British steamed puddings are made with suet, which is the flaky fat around a cow's kidneys. That makes the pudding authentic, but awfully beefy. After playing around with a few versions, I found that using butter and Meyer lemons produces a lovely marmalade-like filling that runs out when it's cut open.

I'm not usually a fan of specialized equipment, but you will need a pudding mold for this. These are metal molds with lids that snap on, usually with latches. They look pretty on a shelf when you aren't using them.

2 cups all-purpose flour, sifted
1½ teaspoons baking powder
½ teaspoon baking soda
½ teaspoon salt
½ pound (2 sticks) unsalted butter, 1 stick frozen, the remaining stick cool but not soft, cut into small pieces

⅓ cup milk
⅓ cup water
½ cup sugar
1 medium Meyer lemon, scrubbed and dried
Whipped cream for serving

Mix the flour, baking powder, baking soda, and salt together in a large bowl. Using the large holes of a box grater, grate the frozen butter into the dry ingredients and mix well. Add the liquids and mix in to a soft dough.

Butter a 3-cup pudding mold well. On a lightly floured surface, roll the dough out to an approximate 10-inch circle. Cut one-quarter of the dough off in a wedge, form it into a circle, and set aside.

Line the mold with the remaining dough, fitting it in nicely. Scatter half of the remaining butter over the dough, press it lightly into the dough, and sprinkle with half the sugar. Prick the lemon all over with a toothpick and set it on top of the butter and sugar. Scatter the rest of the butter over the lemon and add the rest of the sugar.

Top with the pastry lid and pinch tightly to seal the seams. Put on the top of the mold. (If your mold doesn't have a lid, butter a round of parchment paper and cover the top of the pudding, then wrap a piece of aluminum foil over the top of the parchment, and secure the whole thing with a piece of kitchen twine.)

Put the mold on a trivet or a small overturned cup in a large pot, add boiling water to come halfway up the sides of the mold, and cover the pot. Steam gently for 3½ hours. (You will probably need to add more water as the water in the pot evaporates; check the water level about every half hour.)

When the pudding is done, turn it out into a deep dish. Include a slice of crust, a piece of lemon, and plenty of sauce in each serving, and top with a dollop of whipped cream.

Makes 6 to 8 servings

THE THANKSGIVING CHALLENGE

NOVEMBER

THE THANKSGIVING CHALLENGE

by **KIM SEVERSON**

You know how it is with family during the holidays: one smart remark, and someone leaves the table in tears.

It wasn't quite that dramatic at Dining section staff meetings, although we did see one another so much we felt like family.

I was giving a passionate description of the heritage turkey I had ordered for Thanksgiving, a real beauty that had spent nine months running free in a field. I shared that I was feeling conflicted about whether to brine it or stuff it. I opened up. I was vulnerable.

Then Moskin made her flip little comment. "Nobody really cares about the turkey," she said. "It just has to be good enough."

I bit my lip. I tamped down the urge to yell, "I know you are but what am I?" and run from the room in tears. Then I decided to show her how wrong she was. We would prepare Thanksgiving dinner together, with her on the side dishes and me on the bird. Then we'd see.

I believe that from a good turkey, all Thanksgiving flows. Norman Rockwell didn't spend all that time painting pans of sweet potatoes and cranberry sauce, did he? No. He painted turkeys.

From turkey comes stock, the flavor-giving juice that pumps through the entire meal. Good gravy depends on good stock. So does stuffing (more on our stuffing fight in a moment). Delicious turkey does not come from a 29-cent-a-pound supermarket bird with cottony, bland breast meat. Those are, as my favorite turkey breeder says, the Red Delicious apples of turkeys.

A bird that has been bred to thrive in the open develops tastier meat. I've eaten dozens of supermarket and free-range birds, and I will swear to that basic truth on my favorite turkey platter.

There is a catch. Growing a great turkey takes time, and so serving one costs money. But if you can afford it, it's the way to go.

The turkeys from Ayrshire Farm in Upperville, Virginia, spend their days on pasture and get organic feed. Much attention has been paid to their husbandry. They are certified by the Humane Farm Animal Care program. True, they start at $125. But frankly, no expense was too great in proving Moskin wrong.

I wanted a brine so the meat would still be relatively moist even if it was overcooked. The Ayrshire Farm birds spend six hours in a very light brine. But I needed more insurance.

Since I also wanted to avoid water-logged meat and a tub full of saline solution sloshing around in the kitchen, I turned to the collective wisdom of Judy Rodgers at the Zuni Café in San Francisco and a couple of well-respected food editors. Rodgers has had exceptional results salting chickens long before roasting them. Other food publications have used the technique (also called dry-brining) on turkeys with success.

I practiced on a supermarket bird, rubbing in about a half cup of kosher

salt and allowing a couple of days for the salt to draw out moisture and then for the meat to reabsorb it. The turkey was juicy and had an unexpectedly deep, meaty flavor, even though I cooked it longer than I might have liked, to allow for the fact that I had stuffed it.

About that stuffing. Usually, I cook it outside the bird. An unstuffed bird is much more reliable in the oven. It cooks faster. And I've never thought the stuffing was that much better inside.

At this, Moskin scoffed. The stuffing and the bird are parts of a whole, she said. She was shocked that a Thanksgiving purist such as myself would even consider separating them.

But she knew I was uncomfortable stuffing the bird because I didn't want to throw off my roasting times. Was she just trying to goad me into making a Thanksgiving dinner more to her liking? Or was it a trick?

The only solution: make two turkeys.

On our appointed day, I pulled out my Bourbon Red and my American Bronze about an hour before I was going to roast them. I placed some onions, apples, and fresh thyme inside one. The other I gingerly stuffed with a soft dressing made from chanterelles, pancetta, and caramelized pears mixed with Pullman bread.

I pressed what remained into well-buttered tins to create individual stuffing muffins that would be crisp on the outside and steamy-soft inside.

The birds were the talk of the table. OK, some talk was about how the stuffed bird seemed dry. In my defense, it was the smaller one, and I was a little unsure about the interior temperature.

Let me just say: I rocked the stuffing muffins. Imagine how good they must have been, then times it to the tenth power.

Although the softer stuffing cooked in the bird had its fans, it didn't please Little Miss Side Dish. "I think the problem is that you didn't toast the bread," she pointed out between rounds of praise for her curried sweet potatoes and roasted cauliflower.

I didn't run from the table. I didn't cry. I just offered everyone seconds on turkey and passed the gravy. After all, that's what they really wanted.

DRY-BRINED TURKEY

You will need to start the brining process two days ahead.

One 12- to 16-pound turkey, preferably a heritage or pasture-raised bird

About ½ cup kosher salt

1 tablespoon freshly ground black pepper

10 fresh thyme sprigs

½ bunch fresh flat-leaf parsley

2 small onions, halved

2 small apples, cored and halved

8 tablespoons (1 stick) unsalted butter, at room temperature

2 cups water or white wine

Two days before serving, rinse the turkey and pat dry. Rub all over with the salt, slipping salt under the skin where possible and rubbing some into the cavities; use about 1 tablespoon per every 4 pounds of bird. Put the bird in a large plastic bag and refrigerate.

On the second night, turn the turkey over.

A couple of hours before cooking, remove the turkey from the bag and pat dry. Put in a roasting pan and allow to come to room temperature.

Preheat the oven to 450 degrees.

Sprinkle half the pepper into the main cavity of the turkey and add the thyme, parsley, half the onions, and half the apples. Tie the legs together with kitchen twine. Put the remaining apples and onions in the neck opening and tuck the neck skin under the bird.

Rub the butter under the breast skin and over the thigh meat. Sprinkle the bird with the remaining pepper.

Roast for 30 minutes.

Remove the turkey from the oven and reduce the heat to 350 degrees. Cover the breast of the bird and the wing tips with foil. Add 1½ cups water (or white wine) to the roasting pan and roast the bird for another 2 hours or so, depending on size; figure on 12 minutes a pound for an unstuffed bird. Remove the foil from the breast in the last half hour so it browns.

When the turkey has roasted for 2 hours, begin to test for doneness by inserting

an instant-read thermometer (digital is best) into two different places in the thigh, making sure not to touch bone; it should be at about 160 degrees.

When it is done, tip the turkey so the interior juices run into the pan. Remove the turkey to a rimmed baking sheet or a serving platter, cover with foil and then a damp kitchen towel, and allow to rest for at least 30 minutes.

Meanwhile, pour the fat and drippings from the pan into a measuring cup. Add the ½ cup white wine (or broth) to the pan, stirring to deglaze it, and pour that into same measuring cup. The fat and drippings can then be used to make gravy; see page 247.

Makes 10 to 14 servings

TWO-WAY CHANTERELLE AND PEAR BREAD STUFFING

1 large loaf Pullman or other firm white bread
1 pound chanterelle mushrooms
⅓ pound pancetta, cut into small dice
10 tablespoons (1¼ sticks) butter, plus more for the muffin tins
1 large onion, chopped
¼ cup minced shallots (about 3)
Salt and freshly ground black pepper
⅓ cup white wine

3½ cups diced pears (about 4 or 5 ripe firm varieties like Bartlett or Anjou), plus 1 whole pear
1 teaspoon sugar
⅓ cup chopped fresh flat-leaf parsley
¼ cup minced fresh chives
1½ tablespoons finely chopped fresh thyme or 1½ teaspoons dried thyme
2 cups turkey stock, or as needed (chicken broth can be used)

Tear the bread into small pieces (you should have about 16 cups) and put in a roasting pan or large bowl. Cover with paper towels and leave out overnight to dry. Or spread on a baking sheet, in batches, and lightly toast in a 300-degree oven, then put in a roasting pan or large bowl. Set aside.

Wipe the mushrooms clean with a damp towel. Trim the tough ends. Slice some thick, and chop the rest. Set aside.

Put the pancetta in a large skillet and cook over medium heat until the fat is rendered, about 7 minutes. Using a slotted spoon, remove the pancetta to a large plate.

Add 2 tablespoons of the butter to the fat remaining in the pan and turn the heat to medium-high. Add the onion and shallots, season with salt and pepper, and cook, stirring occasionally, until just soft; do not brown. Remove to the plate holding the pancetta.

Add 3 tablespoons butter to the pan, then add the mushrooms, season with salt and pepper, and sauté until starting to brown. Remove to the plate.

Add the wine to the pan and deglaze over medium-high heat, stirring and cooking until the wine reduces by about half. Pour the liquid over the mushrooms.

Wipe out the pan and add the remaining 5 tablespoons butter. Add the diced pears and sugar, in batches if necessary, season with salt and pepper, and sauté until the pears begin to brown slightly. Remove from the heat.

Add the sautéed ingredients to the bread and toss lightly to combine. Add the herbs and toss again. Slowly pour 1 cup of the stock over the mixture and toss. Add enough additional stock to make a very moist stuffing. Taste and adjust for salt and pepper. (If you are stuffing a brined turkey, remember that the juices from the bird will add a bit more salt.)

Preheat the oven to 375 degrees. Generously butter 12 muffin cups.

Just before roasting the turkey, put some of the room-temperature stuffing lightly inside the cavity. Place the whole pear in the opening of the cavity to help hold the stuffing in the bird. Roast as directed.

Fill the muffin cups with the remaining stuffing, pressing down so each one is well filled. Top each with 1 tablespoon stock. Bake for 20 to 30 minutes, until a golden crust forms on the bottom.

To serve, use a butter knife to remove the stuffing muffins and invert onto the plates.

Makes enough stuffing for a 12- to 14-pound turkey and 12 muffins;
if not stuffing a turkey, the recipe will fill 2 dozen muffin cups or a small casserole dish

GRAVY FROM A BRINED BIRD

When I wrote about food for the *San Francisco Chronicle,* we had a lovely test kitchen filled with interns from local cooking schools who did nothing but work on the best ways to cook a million different kinds of dishes. This method for gravy from a brined bird was developed after experimenting with dozens of batches.

4 tablespoons unsalted butter

½ cup all-purpose flour

Pan drippings to taste

½ cup dry white wine (optional)

4 cups homemade turkey stock or low-salt canned chicken broth

Salt and freshly ground black pepper

To make a roux: melt the butter in a large skillet. Add the flour all at once, whisking until incorporated. Cook, whisking occasionally, until the roux begins to look grainy, 3 to 4 minutes. Set aside.

When the turkey is done, pour the pan drippings into a bowl.

Deglaze the roasting pan with the wine by boiling and scraping the pan with a wooden spoon, adding a little water as needed to incorporate the browned bits. Add to the drippings in the bowl. Skim off the fat with a spoon, or refrigerate until the fat has congealed on top, then remove it.

To make the gravy: Bring the broth to a simmer in a covered saucepan, then slowly add 3 cups of the broth to the cold or room temperature roux, whisking constantly. Slowly add the reserved drippings, starting with a few tablespoons; taste, then whisk in more a little at a time until the gravy tastes right to you. Season with salt if needed and pepper. To adjust the consistency, add more broth for a thinner gravy or simmer for a few minutes for a thicker one. Keep warm until ready to serve.

Makes about 4 cups

NOVEMBER

THE THANKSGVING CHALLENGE

---

by JULIA MOSKIN

A person can only take so much.

Every November, Severson likes to chew over the Big Issues: brining versus barding, tenting versus turning, organic versus heritage birds. Her annual quest for a perfect turkey is deeply felt, heroic, and—to my mind—irritating and perverse. Turkey smells good in the oven and looks good on the table, but doesn't it always disappoint on the fork? Isn't it kind of like a 20-pound Yankee Candle, good only for perfume?

She has tried to bring me into the turkey fold with logic ("You just had a turkey sandwich for lunch"), with peer pressure ("Everyone loves turkey"), and with guilt ("These turkeys were slaughtered just for you"). Stringy and tasteless at worst, blandly savory at best, turkey in my opinion achieves greatness only late in life— eaten cold at midnight, slathered with mayonnaise and cranberry sauce and layered between two slices of sour rye bread.

And that's how I disposed of her flesh-covered carcass (I refer to the turkey she roasted, of course) after a tense Thanksgiving cookfight, during which we put the whole meal on the table and let the eaters decide what contributed more to their pleasure: a great turkey-stuffing combo or great side dishes?

I felt my disadvantage keenly. Turkey is the bronzed and golden sun, the star

around which the rest of Thanksgiving revolves. And I adore stuffing. As a cook, however, it gives me no scope. My family recipe is already fixed. It is the One True Stuffing (most people seem to feel the same way), and we are no more likely to change it than to stop interrupting one another at the table.

And so I have to find my thrills and show-off moments in the vegetable kingdom. And when one of those dishes knocks the ball out of the park, as I would venture to say my sweet potatoes with coconut milk and fiery Thai curry paste did at our cookfight dinner, the thrill is that much greater for being unexpected.

Coming up with a new side dish each year while repeating old favorites means that our Thanksgivings have ever more sides. This, more than the turkey, generates a self-indulgent holiday feeling. (I almost wept at the sad tale of a friend whose kitchen-averse family makes only one side dish at Thanksgiving: mashed potatoes or sweet potatoes, never both.)

What other sides could beat the traditional pull of the bird? I brought out an invincible weapon, hidden in the freezer since summer: whole corn kernels, simply tossed in a hot skillet of melted butter and showered with fresh mint when they started to pop and turn brown. I also decided to work on my vegetable-roasting skills.

Not so long ago, Americans were famous for boiling vegetables into submission. In the twenty-first century, we roast every vegetable in sight. But my blast-furnaced specimens often emerge dry, charred, and leathery.

"I never go above 375 degrees in a home oven," counseled one chef, saying that high temperatures dry out the food and brown it too fast. "Vegetables only release that secret buttery sweetness when they turn golden and then brown," she said. A dish of hot water placed in the bottom of the oven when you turn it on produces steamy heat that keeps the vegetables succulent. Using her method and the convection function on my oven, I've achieved roasted vegetable nirvana over and over again.

And I saved a devastating stroke for the dessert course.

"If roast turkey is so good," I said innocently as we ate pumpkin pies, "I wonder why we don't we make it at other times?" You'd think people would serve it at dinner parties, I suggested, embroidering the theme: bohemian-chic restaurants in San Francisco and tongue-in-cheek chefs in Paris would reinterpret it. And yet, strangely, none of those things has come to pass.

I'm just saying.

FIERY SWEET POTATOES

A brilliant variation on classic sweet potato casserole, cribbed from the indispensable Martha Stewart—who could get through the holidays without her?

5 pounds sweet potatoes
1 cup coconut milk
1 tablespoon Thai red curry paste
½ cup packed dark brown sugar
4 tablespoons unsalted butter
1 teaspoon salt

Preheat the oven to 375 degrees.

Put the sweet potatoes on a baking sheet and bake for about 1 hour, until very soft. Remove from the oven.

When the sweet potatoes are cool enough to handle, peel and mash them; put in a large bowl.

Heat the coconut milk with the curry paste in a small saucepan over low heat until hot. Mix the coconut milk mixture, half the sugar, half the butter, and the salt into the potatoes. Set aside until ready to serve, or cover and refrigerate up to 2 days.

About 30 minutes before serving, preheat the oven to 425 degrees.

Put the potatoes in a baking dish, cover with foil, and bake for 20 minutes. Uncover the potatoes, dot with the remaining butter, and sprinkle with the remaining sugar. Turn on the broiler and broil until brown and crusty on top, checking often to prevent scorching.

Makes 10 to 12 servings

ROASTED CAULIFLOWER WITH
LEMON BROWN BUTTER AND SAGE SALT

Cauliflower is my favorite vegetable for roasting, hands down. Scented with lemon and sage, it is positively festive, and with Fiery Sweet Potatoes (page 251), it makes a complete holiday meal for vegetarians.

¼ cup olive oil

¼ cup loosely packed fresh sage
  leaves

1 tablespoon coarse salt

3 heads cauliflower, cored and
  cut into florets

About 1 teaspoon kosher salt

6 tablespoons unsalted butter

Finely grated zest and juice of
  1 lemon

Heat the oil in a small skillet until rippling. Add the sage and cook, stirring, just until crisped, about 2 minutes. Lift out the sage and drain on paper towels. Transfer the oil to a large bowl.

Let the sage cool, then crumble into a small bowl. Stir in the coarse salt; set aside.

Preheat the oven to 375 degrees. Put a roasting pan filled with an inch of water in the bottom of the oven.

Add the cauliflower to the bowl with the sage oil, add the kosher salt, and toss gently until coated. Spread out on two large rimmed baking sheets. Bake for 20 to 30 minutes, until browned. Meanwhile, melt the butter in a small saucepan over medium heat. Once the foam subsides, watch closely and stir often. When the white milk solids on the bottom of the pan are brown and the butter smells toasty, turn off the heat, add the lemon juice, and stir well.

Transfer the cauliflower to a bowl. Pour the butter over, add the lemon zest and half the sage salt, and toss. Taste and season with more of the salt as needed.

Makes 10 to 12 servings

CARAMELIZED CORN
WITH FRESH MINT

Lisa Ades, a magnificent cook and all-around pal, made this for me one late-summer weekend at her house in western Massachusetts, when local corn was in peak season. When I tried to re-create it for Thanksgiving with frozen yellow corn, the dish tasted like airline food. But premium "petite" frozen white corn, which is less sweet, works beautifully when thawed on towels beforehand to draw out the excess liquid.

4 to 5 cups fresh white or yellow corn kernels (from about 12 ears) or two 16-ounce bags frozen white corn

8 tablespoons (1 stick) unsalted butter
½ cup chopped fresh mint
Salt

If using frozen corn, thaw between layers of paper towels, about 30 minutes.

Melt half the butter in a wide skillet over high heat. Add half the corn and cook, stirring often, until golden and browned (the kernels may begin to pop), about 10 minutes. Stir in half the mint and sprinkle with salt. Transfer to a serving bowl and set in a warm spot. Repeat with the remaining corn, butter, mint, and salt.

Makes 10 to 12 servings

STRING BEANS WITH
GINGER AND GARLIC

Every Thanksgiving dinner needs a sparky dish, something bright and snappy, to keep appetites from sliding under the table after the first round of turkey. As a pastrami sandwich needs a pickle, as bollito misto cries out for salsa verde, to me Thanksgiving dinner demands something green and spicy. This Indian dish is my perennial favorite.

2½ pounds green beans (slim haricots verts work especially well), trimmed
¼ cup vegetable oil

¼ cup minced peeled fresh ginger (about a 6-inch piece of ginger)
4 medium garlic cloves, minced
Salt

Bring a large pot of salted water to a boil. Fill a large bowl with ice water. Working in 2 batches, boil the beans until just tender but still crisp and bright green. Start testing after 4 minutes or so, being careful not to overcook them. When they are done, drain and scoop them out with a skimmer, plunge the beans into the ice water to stop the cooking; lift out immediately when cool and drain on kitchen towels. (The beans can be cooked up to a day in advance and kept refrigerated, wrapped in towels.)

When ready to serve, heat 2 tablespoons of the oil in a wide skillet over high heat. Add half the beans, half the ginger, and half the garlic and cook, stirring and tossing constantly, until the beans are heated through and the ginger and garlic are softened and aromatic. Sprinkle with salt and remove to a serving dish. Repeat with remaining oil, beans, ginger, and garlic. Serve.

Makes 10 servings

SPENCERTOWN STUFFING

The writer Maya Angelou has lived a long life and has cooked a lot of turkeys, and one thing she doesn't mince is words. "I think a heavy stuffing makes the turkey feel depressed," she told me in an interview when her first cookbook came out. (She recommends a 3 to 1 ratio of corn bread to white bread to ensure a light mixture.)

In stuffing, as in politics, one American's tradition is another's abomination. I am mindful that our own family recipe, made with great ceremony every year by my uncle Julian Cohen in Upstate New York, would be greeted with horror in many households, as it includes porcini mushrooms, Calvados, raisins, and fresh rosemary. But it is the best there is.

1 cup dried porcini or morel
  mushrooms

2 cups warm water

1 cup Calvados or Cognac

5 tablespoons unsalted butter

3 onions, thinly sliced

Salt

1 large loaf sourdough bread, torn
  into pieces (10 to 12 cups)

¼ cup finely chopped fresh parsley

2 tablespoons finely chopped
  fresh rosemary

2 tablespoons finely chopped
  fresh sage

1 cup applesauce
¾ cup raisins or dried cherries
½ cup coarsely chopped walnuts
   or pecans

1 to 2 cups chicken or vegetable
   broth
Freshly ground black pepper

Soak the mushrooms in the warm water for about 30 minutes, until softened.

Meanwhile, simmer the Calvados in a saucepan until reduced to about ⅔ cup.

Preheat the oven to 375 degrees. Butter a 9-by-13-inch baking dish with some of the butter. (The oven can be anywhere from 350 to 400 degrees if you need to cook both the stuffing and the turkey in it.)

Drain the mushrooms, reserving the liquid. Thickly slice the mushrooms.

Melt the remaining butter in a large skillet. Add the onions and sauté until translucent. Sprinkle with salt if the onions are browning too fast. Add the mushrooms and sauté for 2 minutes. Add the bread, the reserved mushroom liquid, chopped parsley, rosemary, and sage. Stir in the reduced Calvados, applesauce, raisins, nuts, and enough stock so the mixture is moist but not wet. Season to taste with salt and pepper.

Turn out into the buttered baking dish. Bake for 45 minutes to 1 hour, until firm and crusty on top.

Makes 8 to 10 servings

Fried Green Olives
and Garlic Cloves

Deviled Eggs with Cocktail-
Onion Stuffing

Blue Cheese Dip with Toasted
Almonds and Celery Sticks

Tangerine Chicken

Monica's Texas Chili

DECEMBER

THE OPEN-HOUSE CHALLENGE

Candied Cherry Tomatoes

Radish Butter Cups

Andrea's Perfect Ribs

Fried Chickpeas

Cayenne-Sugared Kumquats

Nojitos

THE OPEN-HOUSE CHALLENGE

by **JULIA MOSKIN**

I think Severson may have attended a few too many down-home church suppers and potluck dinners in her youth. As an adult, she has gone to the other extreme when it comes to cooking for a lot of people. She now believes that a party is an excuse to show off with what she calls "small, elegant bites." Among my people, we call this "having to find a place to eat afterwards."

I much prefer bigger, looser party foods: A whole ham everyone can carve from. A bottomless pot of stew or soup with lots of garnishes. Big bowls of nuts, piles of fried olives, and stacks of cookies and clementines.

When a community of people gathered in the past, there was usually something for them to do: raise a barn, sew a quilt, knit socks for the boys overseas. These days, most of us wouldn't know where to start on these worthy projects.

Still, sometimes we want to gather people together and eat. This is a good idea, often immediately followed by a very bad one: potluck.

Please don't have a potluck.

Why not, you ask?

If you are honest, you will admit that the food at potlucks always sucks. Here are just a few reasons: Three bites each of fourteen different dishes does not make a satisfying meal. The main dishes are always cold. Even if you get bossy and tell guests what to make, there will always be too many salads.

A potluck is so much easier, you say.

I can't possibly feed all those people, you whine.

But if you are reading this book, you can have a Stew. My friend Elizabeth is a demon entertainer who didn't let a little hiccup like a divorce stand in the way of a great dinner tradition. As a couple, they had an endearing habit of hosting large dinners called Stews (as it turned out, she did this herself long before they met, so she was able to reclaim the Stew in the divorce). They did it by inviting literally everyone they liked to their house, instructing each guest to bring

one friend and one bottle of wine. They made two enormous pots of stew—three if more than sixty people were expected—such as Texas chili or shrimp curry. There was also an option to please the vegetarians, like vegetable tagine or pasta e fagioli. The stews were made during the week and left in the fridge to think about how to improve themselves. A large batch of brownies was baked the day before the party. Bread, cheese, and fruit were bought on the day, and a huge pot of rice was made just before dinner.

Later on, I sometimes assumed the role of Elizabeth's partner for Stew purposes, and I can attest that it is a low-stress, high-reward way of feeding a large number of loved ones.

What to serve during the pre-Stew hour?

This question brings us to an important modern phenomenon: baby carrots and hummus. These are lovely and nutritious items and they have much to teach us. For today's lesson, the point is that they look totally unappetizing if dumped into a bowl and left as is. In the Middle East, I have never been served hummus that wasn't covered with golden pools of olive oil and dusted with paprika, za'atar, or both. Baby carrots that have been refreshed in water or (even better) cut just before serving really do look crunchy and appealing. Olives that are sprinkled with herbs or fresh lemon zest look better than plain ones.

Having eaten thousands of restaurant meals in my life, I've come to believe that the reason some food looks good to us is that it is carefully made. This registers, subconsciously; even if we don't notice. Good food may not be fancy, but it has to look like someone cared about it.

In a restaurant, we pay to get that feeling. When we invite people over, we offer it for free. Powerful stuff. And isn't that the point?

FRIED GREEN OLIVES
AND GARLIC CLOVES

I found these savory, crispy bites in a cookbook by Simon Hopkinson, an utterly British chef, and immediately adapted them to a Jewish-American holiday. Chanukah is minor on the religious calendar but major in New York City, where competition with Christmas is inevitable.

Deep-frying is traditional for Chanukah because the holiday celebrates light—which, in the time of the Torah, was produced by burning olive oil. The most traditional Chanukah recipes are for doughnuts and fried fish, neither of which have ever appealed to me as a home cook. These do have to be fried at the last minute, but everything else on the menu can be made in advance.

About 36 large garlic cloves
1½ cups pitted green olives, such
  as Manzanilla or Picholine
Vegetable oil for deep-frying
1 cup all-purpose flour
1 teaspoon salt, plus more for
  sprinkling

½ teaspoon freshly ground black
  pepper
3 large eggs
1 cup fresh bread crumbs or
  panko

Put the garlic cloves in a saucepan, cover with cold water, and bring to a boil, then reduce the heat and simmer for 1 minute. Drain and repeat with fresh water. Drain and repeat once more, this time simmering for about 5 minutes, or until the garlic is soft, testing often. Gently lift the garlic cloves out of the pan and drain on paper towels until cool.

Meanwhile, put the olives on paper towels to drain.

When ready to cook, heat 3 inches of oil to 375 degrees in a heavy pot; when the oil is hot enough, a chunk of bread will fry in 30 seconds. Mix the flour, salt, and pepper on a plate. Beat the eggs in a bowl. Spread the bread crumbs on another plate.

Working in batches, roll the garlic cloves and olives in the seasoned flour, then in the beaten eggs, and then in the bread crumbs; repeat the process, and drop into the oil. Cook until golden brown, about 2 minutes. Drain on paper towels and sprinkle lightly with salt. (Let the oil come back to 375 degrees between batches.)

Serve immediately. Or, if you'd rather make them in advance, keep warm in a 200-degree oven for up to 1 hour.

Makes 10 to 12 servings

DEVILED EGGS WITH
COCKTAIL-ONION STUFFING

It is a pain to make deviled eggs, no way around it, but these pay you back. They have a saucy crunch and brininess to them, and like all deviled eggs, they are insanely filling. P.S. If you run with vegetarians, make extra deviled eggs and count them as an entrée.

12 large eggs
3 tablespoons mayonnaise, plus
    more to taste
1 tablespoon Dijon mustard
1 teaspoon cider vinegar
2 tablespoons finely chopped
    cocktail onions, plus brine to
    taste

½ teaspoon cayenne pepper
Smoked paprika for dusting
Finely chopped fresh chives or
    cilantro stems for garnish

Put the eggs in a single layer in a saucepan and cover with cold water by at least 1 inch. Add a teaspoon of salt. Leaving the pot uncovered, turn the heat to high. As soon as the water comes to a boil, turn off the heat and cover.

After 10 minutes, remove the cover and run cold water over the eggs for 1 minute. The eggs can be left to cool in the water for up to 2 hours, or drained and refrigerated for up to 1 week.

To peel the eggs, start at the broader end, where there is an air pocket. Then slice the eggs vertically in half and turn the yolks out into a small bowl.

Add the remaining ingredients (except the garnishes) and mix until smooth. Taste the mixture, adding more mayonnaise and/or onion brine as needed. Scoop the mixture into a thick sealable plastic bag, seal, and chill for at least 1 hour or up to 4 hours. Arrange the whites on a platter, cover, and chill them too.

Just before serving, snip off a small corner of the plastic bag and pipe the filling into the whites. Dust the finished eggs with paprika and shower them generously with herbs.

Makes 24 deviled eggs

BLUE CHEESE DIP WITH
TOASTED ALMONDS AND CELERY STICKS

When Severson and I began working together, we quickly realized that we had been set up. Rather than the shining modern originals we had imagined ourselves, we had clearly been recruited as younger versions of the Dining section's longtime MVPs, Marian Burros and Florence Fabricant. Both women had been at the *Times* for more than twenty-five years and had written about everyone from James Beard to Marcella Hazan before we were born. They taught us so much: how to say "no" to editors, how to stick young reporters with the lunch check, and that there can never be too many recipes for dip.

4 ounces Roquefort or other strong blue cheese	2 teaspoons dry sherry or brandy
½ cup grated white cheddar cheese (sharp or mild)	⅓ cup sliced almonds
1 cup crème fraîche or sour cream	Salt
2 teaspoons fresh lemon juice, or more to taste	Freshly grated nutmeg for dusting
	Celery sticks for serving

Blend the cheeses, crème fraîche, lemon juice, and sherry in a food processor until smooth. Scrape into a container and refrigerate for a few hours, or for up to 2 days.

Just before serving, lightly toast the almonds.

Stir the dip and adjust the seasoning with salt and more lemon juice if needed. Scrape into a serving bowl and dust with nutmeg. Sprinkle the warm toasted almonds over the top and serve with celery sticks.

Makes 2 cups

TANGERINE CHICKEN

It is impossible to explain the virtues of this stew: you have to make it to understand it. But here: it is quick, bright-flavored, sun-colored, and not heavy. Made with supermarket ingredients, it is easy to shop for, but it tastes a bit exotic; in fact, it is a version of a Persian recipe.

The combination of orange and mint sounds like a toothpaste flavor, but somehow they combine in the pot to make a delicate, buttery, fragrant sauce that has people literally scraping at the last drops with heels of bread.

3 tangerines or oranges
4 to 6 tablespoons olive oil
4 pounds boneless, skinless
  chicken thighs
2 onions, minced
4 large garlic cloves, minced
2 tablespoons all-purpose flour
2 cups chicken broth
1½ pounds large carrots, peeled
  and sliced about ¼ inch thick on
  the diagonal

Juice of 1 lemon
1 tablespoon dried mint
Salt and freshly ground black
  pepper
Fresh mint leaves or parsley for
  garnish

Grate the zest from 2 of the tangerines and put in a bowl. Squeeze the tangerine juice into the bowl, discarding any seeds and chunks of pulp.

Heat 2 tablespoons of the oil in a wide skillet until shimmering. Working in batches to avoid crowding the pan, add the chicken and cook on both sides for about 4 minutes until light golden brown. Remove to a plate.

When all the chicken is cooked, add the onions to the pan and adjust the heat so the onions sizzle and cook slowly; stir often to scrape up the browned bits from the bottom. When the onions are golden, add the garlic and sprinkle in the flour, then cook, stirring, for 1 minute, or until fragrant and the flour is no longer raw.

Return the chicken pieces to the pan, then add the broth and about half of the zest/juice mixture. If the liquid doesn't cover the chicken, add water just until it does. Bring to a simmer and simmer until tender, about 45 minutes.

Add the carrots, lemon juice, dried mint, the remaining zest/juice mixture, and salt and pepper to taste. Add zest from the remaining tangerine to taste (some citrus zests have more bitterness than others; you want the flavor to be fresh and orange-bright but not bitter). Simmer until the carrots are very tender, about 20 minutes more.

Serve hot, sprinkled with fresh mint.

Makes 8 to 10 servings

MONICA'S TEXAS CHILI

When I met Monica Waters, I thought the best thing about her was that she had moved to New York City from Austin was to make a documentary film about body waxing. That was before I tasted her chili. No beans. No ground beef. It is as deep and velvety as any French daube, with the added dimension of heat from different kinds of chiles. And, like any recipe that includes several vigorous spices, it tastes even better the day after it is made.

1 tablespoon cumin seeds
1½ teaspoons coriander seeds
3 tablespoons vegetable oil,
  plus more as needed
4 pounds boneless beef chuck,
  cut into 1- to 2-inch cubes
1 large yellow onion, chopped
6 garlic cloves, minced
5 jalapeños, seeded and chopped
3 tablespoons masa harina or
  cornmeal

2 tablespoons pasilla or Chimayo
  chile powder
1 tablespoon dried oregano
One 28-ounce can diced tomatoes
3 dried New Mexico red chiles
One 12-ounce bottle Negro
  Modelo beer
1 ounce unsweetened chocolate
4 cups water

FOR SERVING
Tortillas, Fritos, or Cheese Grits
  (page 28)

Chopped onion
Chopped fresh cilantro

Toast the cumin and coriander seeds in a small heavy skillet over low heat until fragrant. Grind them to a powder in a mortar and pestle or a coffee or spice grinder.

Heat the oil in a large heavy pot over medium-high heat until shimmering. Working in batches to avoid crowding, brown the meat pieces on two or three sides, until very crusty; adjust the heat as necessary to prevent scorching. As it is cooked, remove the meat to paper towels to drain, and add more oil as needed for browning (do not clean out the pot).

To the empty but crusty pot, add the onion, garlic, jalapeños, masa, chile powder, cumin and coriander, and oregano and cook, stirring, until the onion has softened, 5 to 10 minutes.

Add the meat, tomatoes, dried chiles, beer, chocolate, and water. Bring to a simmer and simmer until the meat is fork-tender, about 1½ hours. Remove the dried chiles.

Serve with tortillas, or on top of bowls of Fritos or grits. Sprinkle with chopped onion and cilantro.

Makes 10 to 12 servings

THE OPEN-HOUSE CHALLENGE

by KIM SEVERSON

Here's the thing. I am sometimes clumsy and awk-ward and too polite. I am also enthusiastic and love to eat. Oh, and I don't drink anymore. So one can imagine the dread with which I sometimes approach the cocktail party or the open house or whatever you want to call those events where people stand around and chat and drink and snack.

Please don't misunderstand. I love to stand around and chat and drink and snack. I was made for it. But too often the event can be stiff until people are warmed up with food and alcohol. And even then, they can be awkward and physi-cally formidable.

The social lubrication that alcohol can bring notwithstanding, I blame the food. There is nothing more challenging than a party where one is asked to balance a glass and a tiny plate while attempting to spread something on an awful dry little toast or dip a loosely wrapped spring roll into a peanut sauce before it falls apart, all the while trying to keep up your end of the conversation with a neighbor who is explaining the finer points of environmental theory as it relates to the recession.

And if you factor in all the hand shaking and forced smiling, well, who has a moment to have fun?

That's why I think interesting little bites that can be popped into the mouth with one graceful motion make the best strategy for an open-house menu. Moskin will disagree with this point. Guests ought to be able to make a meal out of an open house, she'll say. They should leave satisfied.

I say, with all due respect, no. Of course you want guests to be satisfied, but a party with food that falls somewhere close to meal level but not quite only confuses everyone. And your mate will undoubtedly be on the prowl to try to get enough to eat, knowing you haven't made dinner plans. Make the dinner plans and take the pressure off!

With a party that is obviously not intended to be dinner, your guests won't feel obligated to stay too long, wondering if everyone is going to make a night of it or whether they are free to have a drink or two, a snack and a sweet, and take their graceful exit.

To that end, I present a menu of small bites that offer punch and interest.

Of course you will have a nicely stocked bar. You might be of a mind to have one specialty cocktail ready to mix and then a few good bottles of white and red wine, or simply a sexy Bandol rosé to pour. Some good local beers and a couple of sophisticated ginger or lemon sodas are nice to have on hand, along with a lot of seltzer. But to really make nondrinkers like me happy, consider a fun specialty cocktail, like my no-jitos. (And please don't call them mocktails. That just makes us recovering drunks feel mocked.)

For food, start with cherry tomatoes dipped in a candy glaze tart with balsamic vinegar. Sesame seeds and salt offer a savory counterpoint. Radishes and butter are a terrific combination, and here I punch them up with anchovy-herb butter piped into the

little radish cups. Those, along with the remarkable candied kumquats, can all be made a day ahead of time to allow you plenty of time to get the house ready.

The only things you'll need to make during the party are the fried crispy chickpeas with the smoky bite of piménton, which you can do in a few batches as the party progresses, and the ribs.

Now, I realize ribs take more than a bite or two to consume, but they can be eaten with one hand and are hearty enough to satisfy Moskin, who undoubtedly has neglected to make dinner plans and expects you to feed her.

CANDIED CHERRY TOMATOES

The idea for these came from Serious Eats, a New York City website started by Ed Levine, the menschiest old food guy around. His team of young, smart cooks put the recipe together for Rachael Ray, a friend who cleverly put it in an issue of her magazine. It is brilliant, because the tomatoes come with their own little dressing jackets. They are a bit fussy to make but well worth the conversation they will spark.

¼ cup white and black sesame
   seeds, toasted (about 2
   tablespoons each)
1 teaspoon salt
2 cups sugar

⅔ cup balsamic vinegar
1 cup light corn syrup
24 firm ripe cherry tomatoes,
   stems removed

Line a rimmed baking sheet with parchment. Put the sesame seeds and salt in a small bowl, mix, and set aside.

Clip a candy thermometer to the side of a deep 3- to 4-quart saucepan. Combine the sugar and balsamic vinegar in the pan and boil over medium-high heat, swirling the pan occasionally, until the sugar is dissolved. Stir in the corn syrup.

Continue to cook, brushing down the sides of the pan with a moistened pastry brush to prevent crystallization and adjusting the heat as needed so the syrup doesn't boil over, until the syrup registers 305 degrees (hard-crack stage) on the thermometer. Remove from the heat.

Put a toothpick into the stem end of a tomato, then dip the tomato into the syrup, allowing the syrup to go a little over halfway up the tomato. Twirl gently and carefully over the pan to let the excess drip off, then immediately dip the bottom half of the tomato into the sesame seeds and stand, seed end down, on the lined baking sheet. Repeat with the remaining tomatoes, reheating the sugar syrup over low heat as needed to restore fluidity.

Let cool for 10 minutes at room temperature before serving.

Makes 24 tomatoes

RADISH BUTTER CUPS

Butter and radishes make perfect sense. The sweet cream of the butter is soft against the sharp crisp spice of the radish. Adding anchovies and herbs elevates this combination into party-worthy status.

2 bunches round radishes (you might have to buy a few bunches to get 20 radishes of roughly equal size—this a party after all, and visuals matter)

2 anchovy fillets

½ pound (2 sticks) of the best salted butter you can find, softened but still cool

2 tablespoons chopped fresh flat-leaf parsley

2 tablespoon chopped fresh chives

5 gherkins, finely chopped

½ teaspoon freshly lemon juice

Fleur de sel or other great finishing salt

Slice the top and tail off each radish, so they will sit on a platter without tilting or rolling. Using a small melon scoop, a serrated grapefruit spoon, or a paring knife, remove some of the white center from each one to form a small bowl. Put them in ice water while you make the anchovy butter.

Mash the anchovies well in a medium bowl. Mix in the butter and everything else but the salt.

Fold a square of waxed paper or plastic wrap. The idea is to make a shape that can open into a cone. Spoon the soft butter into the cone, snip off the tip, and pipe butter into each radish. Sprinkle with salt and serve.

Makes 20 bites

ANDREA'S PERFECT RIBS

I once spent a magical evening with Andrea Reusing, the chef at Lantern Restaurant in Chapel Hill. She has a musician husband, two great kids, and a way of making food delicious, interesting, and uncomplicated. I want to be her, except for the husband part. She showed her skill in her book *Cooking in the Moment*, which I wrote about; it's where I discovered this recipe. These will go fast. You might want to make extra.

2 racks small spareribs (about 5 pounds total)
2 tablespoons vegetable oil
2 dried hot chiles, such as árbol
1 tablespoon fennel seeds
Kosher salt and freshly ground black pepper

Preheat the oven to 450 degrees.

Rub the ribs with the oil. Grind the chiles and fennel in a clean spice or coffee grinder, until evenly ground and slightly coarse, but not pulverized. Rub all over the ribs, then give the ribs a good seasoning with salt and pepper.

Put on a rack set over a rimmed baking sheet and roast for 15 minutes.

Reduce the heat to 375 degrees and roast for another 1 hour and 15 minutes or so, until the ribs are golden and tender. Let rest for about 5 minutes.

Cut the ribs apart between the bones and arrange on a platter.

Makes about 24 ribs

FRIED CHICKPEAS

These are a perfect nibble. Although you will have to tend to the stove for a bit, you can do it during the last of your preparations for the party or make batches as they run out. Lime zest works well too, but I like the slight sweetness of the orange zest.

2 teaspoons smoked paprika
1 teaspoon cayenne pepper
½ teaspoon kosher salt
6 tablespoons extra virgin
  olive oil

Two 15-ounce cans chickpeas,
  drained, rinsed, and thoroughly
  dried
2 teaspoons grated orange zest

Combine the paprika, cayenne, and salt. Set aside.

Heat the oil in a large skillet until very hot but not smoking. Add about half the chickpeas and cook, stirring frequently, until crisp—this takes about 15 minutes. Transfer to paper towels to drain while you cook the second batch.

Put the chickpeas in a serving bowl, sprinkle with the paprika mixture, and toss to coat. Sprinkle with the orange zest, give them one more toss, and serve.

Makes about 3 cups

CAYENNE-SUGARED KUMQUATS

I first had these at a cocktail party at Michael Bauer's house. He is the longtime executive food editor and restaurant critic for the *San Francisco Chronicle*, and it was as part of his crew in the late 1900s and early 2000s that I really learned to cook. He also throws impeccable parties. This recipe relies on excellent, thin-skinned kumquats, which you can now have shipped to your door if you can't find them. California's Ojai Valley is a good place to look. These offer an amazing bite of heat, sweet, and tart all at once.

3 tablespoons sugar	2 egg whites
1½ teaspoons cayenne pepper	30 kumquats, preferably
¼ teaspoon salt	thin-skinned

Stir together the sugar, cayenne, and salt. Whisk the egg whites in a small bowl until foamy and smooth.

Dip each kumquat halfway into the egg whites and let the excess drip off, then dip in the sugar mixture and set on a rack to dry. These will keep for a couple of days between layers of waxed paper in a plastic container at room temperature.

Makes 30 bites

NOJITOS

I like a cocktail without booze or too much sugar but with plenty of bite. This is festive and delicious, and will make the people at your party who don't want to drink feel refreshed, cared for, and happy.

12 small fresh mint leaves, plus a
  mint sprig for garnish
2 tablespoons fresh lime juice
1 tablespoon superfine sugar

¼ teaspoon grated peeled ginger
  (use a Microplane)
½ cup club soda or seltzer
Lime slice

Muddle (mash) the mint leaves with the lime juice, sugar, and ginger in a cocktail shaker. Add ice cubes to fill the shaker and pour in the club soda. Gently shake a few times to incorporate.

Strain into a tall cocktail glass filled with ice. Garnish with the mint sprig and lime slice.

Makes 1 cocktail

INDEX

Note: Page references in *italics* refer to photographs of recipes.

Fish (*continued*)

    Smoked Salmon and Cucumbers with Raspberry Vinaigrette, 108

Frittata with Caramelized Onions and Sherry Vinegar, 122–23

Fritters, Corn, 170, *171*

Fruit. *See also specific fruits*

    Dried, Drop Scones, Bill Yosses', 216–17

G

Garlic

    -Anchovy Dressing, Escarole Salad with, *18,* 19

    Cloves and Green Olives, Fried, *263,* 263–65

    and Ginger, String Beans with, 256

    Greasy Spaghetti, 102

Ginger

    Bacon-Fat Gingersnaps, *220,* 221

    and Cereal-Milk Panna Cotta, 45

    Dark Molasses Gingerbread, 11, *11*

    and Garlic, String Beans with, 256

    Nojitos, 283

    Spice "Beat Moskin" Toffee-Kissed Cookies, 233

Gingerbread, Dark Molasses, 11, *11*

Gingersnaps, Bacon-Fat, *220,* 221

Goat Cheese–Nori Spread, Spicy, Homemade Sesame Crackers with, 40–41

Gougères, Cheddar, *16,* 17

Grains

    Bazargan (Cracked Wheat Salad with Pomegranate Dressing), 155–56, *156*

Cheese Grits with Scallions, Bacon, and Red Pepper, 28–29

    Farro Salad, *134,* 135–36

Grape(s)

    Concord, Pie, *186,* 187–89

    Red, Mozzarella, and Black Olive Salad, 121

Gravy from a Brined Bird, 247

Greasy Spaghetti, 102

Greens

    The Best Kale Salad, 86

    Caesar Salad in a Cup, *54,* 54–55

    Dinner Salad with Mustard-Shallot Vinaigrette, Eggs, and Garlic Toast, 205–6

    Escarole Salad with Anchovy-Garlic Dressing, *18,* 19

    Green-Salad Soup, 154

    Italian Green Salad with Vinaigrette, 98

    Kale Chips, 132

    Spaghetti Pie, 207–8

Green-Salad Soup, 154

Grits, Cheese, with Scallions, Bacon, and Red Pepper, 28–29

H

Ham Biscuits, *51,* 51–53

Herbs. *See also specific herbs*

    Italian Salsa Verde, 182, *182*

I

Ice cream

    Tangerine-Vanilla Floats, 22, *22*

Italian Green Salad with Vinaigrette, 98
Italian Salsa Verde, 182, *182*

J

Jam, Quick, with Frozen Strawberries, *52,* 53
Jam Biscuits, *51,* 51–53
Julia Child's Tomato Sauce, 167–68

K

Kale
  Chips, 132
  Salad, The Best, 86
Kumquats, Cayenne-Sugared, 281

L

Lamb Rack with Cilantro-Mint Crust, 76
Lemon
  Brown Butter and Sage Salt, Roasted Cauliflower with, 252
  –Brown Butter Shortbread, 175–76, *176*
  Cheese Layer Cake, *58,* 58–59
  Meyer, Pudding, Steamed, 234–35
  Salt, Potato Chips with, 63
  Zest and Green Apples, Fennel Salad with, 75
Limes
  Mint and Cucumber Soda, 131
  Nojitos, 283
  Pho, 42–43

Pink Peppercorn Cocktails, 39
Skirt Steak with Spicy Cucumber Salad, 172–73
Liver, Chicken, Pâté, 85

M

Macaroni
  and Cheese, Crusty, 31
  and Cheese Pancakes, 65
Main dishes
  Andrea's Perfect Ribs, 279
  Boeuf Bourguignon with Chive Mashed Potatoes, 32–33
  Dinner Salad with Mustard-Shallot Vinaigrette, Eggs, and Garlic Toast, 205–6
  Dry-Brined Turkey, 242–43, *243*
  Frittata with Caramelized Onions and Sherry Vinegar, 122–23
  Grilled Flank Steak, *180,* 181
  Janet's Pasta, 197
  Lamb Rack with Cilantro-Mint Crust, 76
  Monica's Texas Chili, 271–72
  The Moskin Method for Pasta, 203–4
  Not My Grandmother's Brisket, 111–12
  Pasta with Roast Chicken, Currants, and Pine Nuts, 20, *21*
  Picnic Fried Chicken, *142,* 143
  Pork Braised in Milk and Cream, 87–89, *88*
  Prime Rib with Popovers, 96–97
  Refrigerator Chicken, 209
  Roast Chicken in a Pot, 194–95
  Rosemary-Cornflake Chicken, 109–10